Learning to Lead

Also available from Continuum

50 Life Skills to Ensure Kids Stay in School, Off Drugs and Out of Trouble –
David Becker

Handbook of Creative Learning Activities – Steve Bowkett

101 Essential Lists on Managing Behaviour in the Secondary School – Alex
Griffiths and Pauline Stephenson

Building Classroom Success – Eliminating Academic Fear and Failure –
Andrew Martin

Learning to Lead

Using leadership skills to motivate students

Graham Tyrer

**Resources to accompany this book are available online at:
www.continuumbooks.com/resources/9781441155726**

Please visit the link and register with us to receive your password and to access these downloadable resources.

If you experience any problems accessing the resources, please contact Continuum at: info@continuumbooks.com

continuum

Continuum International Publishing Group

The Tower Building
11 York Road
SE1 7NX

80 Maiden Lane, Suite 704
New York, NY 10038

www.continuumbooks.com

British Library Cataloguing-in-Publication Data
A catalogue record for this book is available from the British Library.

ISBN: 978-1-4411-5572-6 (paperback)

Library of Congress Cataloging-in-Publication Data
Tyrer, Graham.
Learning to lead / Graham Tyrer.
  p. cm.
ISBN 978-1-4411-5572-6 (pbk.)
1. Educational leadership. 2. School management and organization.
3. Organizational learning. I. Title.

LB2805.T97 2010
370.1—dc22

Typeset by Ben Cracknell Studios
Printed and bound in Great Britain by Cromwell Press

Contents

Foreword

'Pupil voice' has rightly emerged as a vital ingredient in discussions about the next stage of 'school improvement' and it features strongly in debates about the future of schooling. Like so many 'taken for granted' desirables, the detail of what's involved is often assumed rather than spelled out.

Charles Handy* once put his finger on why pupil voice is most elusive in the 11–16 secondary school when he compared primary pupils with 'workers' who were always busy with tasks to complete, and sixth formers with clients who made choices about what they would and wouldn't do. By contrast, he suggested, 11–16 pupils were neither 'workers' nor 'clients': they were more like the cars on the assembly line with different people giving them a bit of physics followed by maths then art, etc. as the timetable and the years passed until they are released after GCSE.

Of course his imagery was fanciful but it has sufficient truth in it to strike a chord and perhaps to explain why in the difficult adolescent years when the school's concern for discipline and conformity gets in the way of developing pupil responsibility and leadership. School Councils are so often as far as it gets, and then the participants are predictable in their backgrounds and their influence on school life is marginal. Some schools, however, have gone further and involved pupils not just in specific leadership initiatives but also enabled them to influence departments and faculties as well as engage in leading learning and having a real say in every aspect of school life.

Graham Tyrer has led such a school and his book will inspire those who would like to take this issue seriously, as surely everybody must who wishes to create schools which come closer to unlocking the minds and opening the shut hearts of many more of their students.

Tim Brighouse, Commissioner for London Schools and visiting Professor at the Institute of Education at London University, UK

*Handy, C. (1984) *Taken for Granted? Looking at Schools as Organisations*, Longman

Introduction

I have written this book for colleagues in schools and children's services who would like to help young people learn leadership skills. It's my experience that the more we explicitly teach leadership, the more young people want to improve their own behaviour and the behaviour of others in their class, year group, school and community.

So this book is for headteachers, senior leaders in schools and children's services, class teachers, youth workers, special education needs coordinators, year heads, leaders of personal, health and social education, citizenship, and anyone with an interest in improving young people's motivation and inclusion.

The book is a set of activities which have been tried and tested in schools. All the activities can be used on their own and adapted for the needs of your lessons.

They can be also be taught as a planned course in leadership, delivered in or out of school time. You'll find online an example of how the activities can be planned as a series of ten one-hour workshops (see online resource 'Building a team workshop'). This is a real plan I use in the schools I work in to improve the behaviour of groups of young people. Students all have the potential to lead themselves and others. Some use this potential well and others do not: teaching students how to lead gives them a focus, direction and improves their leadership skills.

It's been my experience that school improvement is both gained and secured when students feel they have helped lead rising standards. Helping students learn how to lead brings out of them the ability to teach others in class, address assemblies, talk at staff meetings, take a more productive role in family and community life, lead their school councils and think more positively about themselves. Increasingly, the world of higher education and employment will require of our young people that they have the skills of innovation, enterprise and leadership. This book is a response to that need.

I've designed the activities around a group of specific leadership skills. These skills are those I have found make a difference to young people's capacity to lead themselves and others:

- using personal integrity
- deciding what personal values are and sticking to them
- being better organized so students are able to make a difference
- being ambitious both for themselves and others
- having the skills to give instructions to others
- guiding others in a way that encouragement is offered
- setting an example and not being afraid to act as a role model
- being able to ask questions effectively
- taking a longer-term view of things
- seeing beyond the present moment
- showing courage and determination
- inspiring the trust of others
- empathizing with others to lead them in a positive direction.

I have also included examples of how to set personal and group challenges. These are exciting opportunities for students to make a positive difference in their own lives and the lives of others. They can allow students to put into practice the leadership skills they have been learning.

Throughout the book you'll see the views of young people who have been taught leadership. Some of these students knew they had leadership skills at the start and others were surprised to find this potential. Michael, aged 14, said: 'When I was asked to take part in a leadership course I was really curious. I had never thought of myself as a leader. But then, after a while, I could see that maybe I was. I began to help people in the learning to lead group and even help people work better in their lessons. I did more at home too, and my parents noticed. My mum even came to a conference I was invited to and told everyone how well I'd done and how much I'd changed.'

It is my belief that learning to lead is essential if students are to get the most out of their learning in and out of school. This book has a range of activities to encourage you and your students as you develop their leadership potential and enhance the learning opportunities of everyone in your community.

There are so many people who have played a key role in pioneering this work. I particularly want to thank the students and staff at Nicholas Chamberlaine Technology College and Ash Green School and Arts College in Warwickshire, and also the staff and students at Chenderit School in Northamptonshire. Students in all three of these schools are represented in the student voice sections of this book. I would also like to thank Dr Jane McGregor and Professor Wendy Robinson who helped evaluate the success of the work.

If you or your school would like training in how to develop a course in leadership teaching, feel free to contact me through my website www.grahamtyrer.com. I have delivered learning to lead training to the National College for School Leadership, the Specialist Schools and Academies Trust and a range of local authorities and individual schools. Some schools have developed leadership learning with whole year groups, some with individual classes. All have told me that this has made a positive difference: students have become more engaged, more responsible, more willing to help lead the school. I'd be delighted to design bespoke training for you and your students in how to help students learn how to lead. Although this book gives you everything you need to teach learning to lead in your school.

Part 1

The Beginning

1   Why leadership?

I've found teaching about leadership to be a gateway into the kinds of responses we most want in our schools. Students want to be trusted and challenged, even when it looks as though they don't. Leadership gives them a sense that they are worth something, that they have things to offer, and that their experiences can be useful and helpful to others. Just about every student has this capacity. How do I know? Even the most disruptive, difficult students show leadership qualities – they're just not in the right direction yet. We've all seen them: the class clowns, hijacking the lessons, challenging for the helm so they can lead things in the direction they want and not the teacher's. They want to be liked and respected by their friends; they want other people to laugh with them and admire their control.

This is why I started teaching leadership: a sense that all leadership potential was being wasted, and channelled away from success, achievement and reward. I wondered what would happen if we made a conscious, structured, direct effort to transform this negative energy into something positive. I wondered what you would have to teach, what the curriculum would be, how you could engage and motivate students so that they believed they had the capacity to change themselves and others without losing face, while still keeping the image of 'cool' that they so keenly seek. I wondered: what if we showed so many students they had positive leadership abilities, taught them how to use these abilities and then got them to teach others, what would happen?

To say teaching students to lead has been rewarding is an understatement. I've seen learning to lead students do better in their tests and exams than similar students who didn't learn leadership. Some have led a county conference for young leaders, public speaking to hundreds of their peers and lead workshops about leadership. Others have gone to local businesses and discussed their ideas about leadership and motivation with managing directors and shopfloor leaders. While yet others have debated in the House of Commons about the future of their area with their local MP. Others have attended the National College for School Leadership, which trains teachers and students in how to set up and run leadership classes. Many have helped me run workshops for the local authority's (LA's) headteachers and given presentations about their work to all the county's inspectors and the chief education officer.

That's all on the grand scale. It's just as, if not more, important to see find them making a difference in the classroom, in the corridor and in their local community. Students asking their teachers at the start of the lesson, 'Is there anything I can do to help today? Who do you want me to sit next to and help?' Even taking responsibility for a corridor notice board, finding the resources from the right teachers, discussing the display, maintaining it and getting staff feedback requires leadership. When students see themselves as potential leaders they rethink the concept of involvement in their community. They move from a sense that leadership is for other people, to a feeling that schools are places of opportunity. The future is theirs to determine. They can either lead or be led. At the very least, we owe it to our students to give them the choice.

2 What the students have to say

Natali – Student voice

We researched what the future will be like. This is what we found out might happen by 2040 when we will be adults. One of our leadership activities was to think: 'Is this the future we want?' If it isn't, we have to make another one and we have to lead it, not follow. If we like this vision, we have to be part of it so we can own it and make it ours. Leadership is about this: being part of things. Not being a spectator, being a player, working with others and not being afraid to take control if it helps others.

- Insect-like robots used for crop pollination, 2012.
- ID cards replaced by biometric scanning, 2015.
- Nanobots in toothpaste attack plaque, 2020.
- Thought recognition becomes everyday input, 2025.
- First Bionic Olympics, 2030.
- Emotion-control chips used to control criminals, 2030.
- Moon base the size of a small village is built, 2040.

We have found that learning about leadership increases confidence, attainment and a sense that you have control over your life. It increases the sense that we learn best in a community whose members takes responsibility one for another.

Aadarsh – Student voice

When I started learning to lead I didn't think I could change things. I thought things just happened to me. It's different now. I want to make changes. I can see where they need to be made. I can sit in a lesson and think: how can I make things better? How can I help someone do their best, get better grades, behave better?

Tatyana – Student voice

I knew I could do it. But I didn't know how it worked. I couldn't talk about how I led people. I wasn't even sure I wanted to. You've just got to try. I worked with a group of primary school students on a gifted and talented project. We involved the National Space Centre. I helped the young students see what they had to offer and build teams together. There's nothing more exciting than helping other people do what they didn't think they could.

Katy – Student voice

I remember standing up in front of a room full of headteachers and thinking: they are just people like me. There's nothing to be afraid of. So I started speaking. I had rehearsed and everything, so I knew it would be all right. And it felt good telling people about leadership because I knew how to lead well. I knew it was about trust and thinking about other people. It's about having confidence to believe in yourself and not be afraid.

Michael – Student voice

When I first started, I thought: Why me? Have I got leadership qualities? I'm so quiet. But then I began to see that it isn't about shouting and being bossy. That doesn't get you anywhere. It's about setting a good example and being yourself. You have seen what's best for everybody: in the corridor, in the classroom or on the playground. And you can change other people too. It doesn't happen quickly but it does happen. When I first said to someone, 'You can be better than you are now.' They said 'Why and what's the point?' But I kept at it because it doesn't happen really quickly. Now they ask, 'When do I change?' not why.

3 Leadership is about the future

Why do we learn? So that we can lead the future. Does this sound too large a claim? It shouldn't. When Year 9 students motivate themselves to teach a class of Year 6 students and evaluate the experience – finding out what the students want to learn, how they learn best and then marshal the required resources – they are leading other students to become more effective learners, and in an obviously significant manner. So can all students do this? Yes, perhaps not immediately but with explicit teaching they can plan for their own and others' progress in a focused manner. Leadership isn't always so high profile. Setting an example to others by, for example, lining up for a lesson, quietly and responsibly is an act of leadership. It requires thinking of others, seeing the bigger picture, being ambitious and wanting to improve your skills.

We know the future will be full of opportunities and challenges. The young people who will best be able to face this with confidence will have the leadership skills to build teams, be honest about themselves and imaginatively change the world around them. You will either **make change** or **change will make you**. Too many young people think that they have no influence or capacity to plan, create and innovate. Learning to lead helps them see it doesn't have to be like this. By the time five terms of learning leadership have been completed, most young people say they feel more able to plan, structure and develop their lives.

You can teach leadership in a concentrated burst of a week or two, but it needs all day, every day for this to have an effect, and it can be profound immersion learning.

Most schools have taken their time in teaching leadership and nurtured many small changes, allowing for the normal 'three steps forward, one back' characteristic of learning.

Students change their understanding of leadership. They see it is for them, about them and within their reach. Most students starting the course think they aren't leaders. Part of the work is to convince them that they have this potential.

4 The future will require high order leadership skills

More and more employers are telling us that students who show initiative, take responsibility and can work well in a team have the edge in the rapidly changing work environment. Higher education colleagues stress the importance of self-directed, interdependent learners. Explicit teaching of leadership skills shows students that they have the potential to take advantage of the future rather than passively waiting for it.

5 Leadership is for everyone

There are so many aspects to life in and out of school that require leadership: peer mentoring, peer assessment, chairing group work, taking posts of responsibility, planning and organizing your own work, and engaging with a lesson. Just about every aspect of school and community life opens up leadership opportunities. Rarely, however, is leadership explicitly taught. It's too often thought to be for someone else: it's part of the National Professional Qualification for Headship (NPQH), it's only for prefects or teachers, headteachers or entrepreneurs. But leadership is for everyone. It's about helping students to take responsibility for others around them. It's about helping them to motivate themselves to achieve more and see learning as relevant. Leadership teaching shows students that they can improve the way they learn, improve their self-esteem and feel more in control of the events around them. Student participation in school life is so important if we are to be serious about inclusion. Imagine classrooms where students say: 'I know why I want to learn, I know how to construct a learning activity and I can help others to lead their own learning more effectively.' Showing students that they all have leadership potential and that they can improve their skills over time, helps build a more responsive, dynamic learning organization.

So, what if all students:

- saw themselves as potential leaders?
- saw themselves as responsible for others in their lessons?
- designed **personal challenges** to improve their own or someone else's learning?
- designed, delivered, evaluated and assessed a **group challenge** to improve the lives of others in their school or wider community?
- knew so much about learning that they were able to research effective teaching and learning in their own and other schools and make recommendations for improvement to governing bodies, school leadership teams and staff meetings?

And what if schools:

- planned **leadership learning** into their curriculum as part of citizenship or the pastoral programme?
- offered **leadership as an extended learning opportunity**?
- designed **leadership certification with universities, chambers of commerce or their LA** to give students? Thus increasing their employability and sense of self-esteem.

6 What leadership means

For learning to lead, we define leadership as the following skills:

Positive influence over others

Give instructions to help a group task

Students should be courteous, polite and yet assertive when giving instructions. Often students believe leaders to be 'bossy'. Help them to see that this is not so. There are three key aspects to giving instructions.

Say 'thank you' rather than please after an instruction. Try to use the name of the person you are talking with. Establish a personal link; don't sound like you are begging, but that you expect the instruction to be carried out.

Have clarity of vision: when you describe the instruction, clearly explain the objective. Try to depersonalize the outcome. So, 'It's important to pick that litter up, thanks.' Rather than, 'I'd like you to pick the litter up.' The other person isn't doing the job for you. He or she is doing it because it's important, socially or morally.

Explain the positive outcomes for the greatest number of people. Say, 'when we do this, we'll all be better off, the school will get more money because visitors will be impressed'. It's important also not to use a conditional: it's not a matter of 'if we do this'. Assume it will be done – this is part of assertive leadership.

Guide other people

Examples of this include: find out where other people are. Get alongside their views, their hopes and fears. 'I know what you're going through. I can't change it. But I would like to help you.' You don't take away the worry and anxiety of others. You help them do this themselves. Guiding isn't telling. It's giving the other person the skills and confidence to grow.

Question to secure a task objective

Use 'we' when asking questions; use open questions; and use closed questions when you want to build confidence. So what do we want to achieve? Get the group to 'sign up' to an objective, but make sure it's one everyone wants to achieve, and be clear that an outcome is important:

'We are going to design a radio programme for Year 6 students.'

'What changes do we expect to come and must there be changes otherwise are we wasting our time?'

'What three things do we do we most need?' (Closed question to get others agreeing what skills, materials and people will be important to get a job done.)

'What will things look like when we are finished?' (Agree a shared vision.)

Set an example

We say: 'Try to be excellent; turn up on time; do your homework; don't miss lessons; get your work in on time.' We are an example to others. Having role models explain this is so important. We find alumni of the school who have had some success. This can be in business, social or religious contexts. Ex-students who have 'made it' have the ability of connecting school success with success in later life. A builder, who had made significant financial success, came along and connected the processes of school life with his business. He talked about what time he got to work, how being early set an example for his colleagues, how being on time for a meeting gained an advantage with those he was dealing with, and how being meticulous with his paperwork got things done faster and helped him keep ahead of his competitors.

Take a longer-term view of things
Activity

Encourage students to do the following: 'Think of the next hour, the next day, the next week. Take yourself forward in your imagination in small steps. Even to the end of the lesson.' Have leaders write the word 'plenary' at the start of their lesson then write, in the present tense, how the lesson will go. 'I'm helping someone else. I'm helping myself. I'm helping the teacher. I feel good that I've kept myself focused. I am polite and consider the thoughts of others.'

> Teach student leaders that having a positive self-image makes it more likely they will behave in a confident and optimistic manner.

These brief lesson affirmations have great power if repeated and used often. It becomes a key leadership routine, to see the lesson as you want it to be. So when we think through the personal challenge, we encourage students to envision the future they want to have. We say: 'The stronger this vision is, the more 'gravity' it has, the more it will draw you on.'

Take the initiative

Be the first to step up, to make a suggestion, or to think of an idea. **You can't break an idea. You can only silence it.** And a silent idea is powerless.

Activity

Encourage students to be the first to put their hand up if they don't understand a lesson or a teacher's explanation. Taking the initiative is about looking after yourself. Role play this for five or ten minutes. One of the students is the teacher. Say: 'When you put up your hand, you're voting for your future. And you're leading others who haven't got the confidence to see themselves as a leader of their learning.'

Show courage and determination

Leadership requires courage: the courage to stand up for someone in trouble, to deal with a personal problem, asking for help if necessary; the courage to be a role model.

Activity: safely face your worries

Ask students to think of two events in life they find difficult. They can make them up if they want to. Put these in a secret box anonymously. Then forum theatre them as a whole group, picking out situations at random. The teacher plays a key role, inviting suggestions and pauses from the group so that others can get involved with better routes or solutions.

Inspire the trust of others

For leaders to make change and influence others, they have to create an unspoken social contract with those they lead. This is made up of at least four parts: what you **believe**; what you **say**; how you **behave**; and how you **listen**.

Activity: the balance of trust

Two leaders stand back to back. They slowly move their feet away from each other while still staying balanced. Eventually they are so balanced they depend on each other for support.

Empathize with others

Leaders have to be able to feel what others feel in order to lead them. This can run counter to students' initial intuitions about leadership.

Activity: thought shadowing

Model the role play first. Label three students: A, B and C. A is a new student to the school. B is the person sitting next to her at break time. B is difficult to talk to, has his own set of friends, and doesn't want to be welcoming. C is the 'real thoughts' of A. After a few minutes of the drama beginning, quiz C about the real thoughts of A. C replies in role as the feelings and thoughts of A.

After students have tried this, draw together by explaining that the skill C students have demonstrated is empathy: they have had to feel something of the exclusion and need for friendship A went through in role. Discuss a situation when, say, a family member has needed help, with reading or homework or bullying at school. To help him, you have to imagine being him. Leaders who do not do this, think only of themselves and that becomes being 'bossy'.

If you can, get someone from the school hierarchy to be interviewed by the group about times when she has had to use empathetic skills to lead. Devise a role play job interview where the headteacher, in role as himself, has to help a candidate for a teaching post feel at ease and thoughtful. Discuss the paralinguistic of, for example, the 45 degree seating angle to minimize pressure, using eye contact but not staring; a tone of voice assertive but not overpowering.

Organize others

Leaders have to step up when others won't; leaders have to put the interests of others first, even before their own.

Activity: a factory in crisis

An easy teacher in role: using play money, pay the 'workers' for their day's production. Ask them how their day has been, whether there is anything they need. Build an imaginative bond between them and the 'factory'. Cut to the next day. This time give them half the money for the same work; explain how sorry you are, but that's all you can afford and leave the drama. Narrate like this: 'The workers didn't go home straight away. They stayed in the canteen. There was silence, until one of them said: . . .' and let them stay in role as a group for about ten minutes.

It doesn't matter what 'story' emerges. There's plenty to reflect on and learn through. If strong leadership emerges, so be it. If there is incoherence and division, talk through why, how the organization of the staff could have been improved, even if simply to get negotiations going with the factory owner.

Positive influence over yourself
Using your personal integrity

Encourage students to have three values posted into their planners. Put ten key values of leadership (see the list below) on a PowerPoint slide, as a leader language display, and begin the next activity.

Activity

Use the following list of values, starting with ten (any ten) and letting it grow through discussion and having the students research between classes.

- Achievement
- Adventure
- Affection
- Arts
- Community
- Competition
- Cooperation
- Country
- Creativity
- Democracy
- Ecological awareness
- Effectiveness
- Excellence
- Fame
- Friendships
- Helping other people
- Helping society
- Honesty
- Independence
- Integrity
- Involvement
- Knowledge
- Loyalty
- Money
- Nature
- Personal development
- Privacy
- Recognition
- Religion
- Reputation
- Responsibility
- Security
- Self-respect
- Serenity
- Stability
- Status
- Truth
- Wealth
- Wisdom

Activity

Write the above words onto cards and have the class stand, holding them in groups of five, for a volunteer 'values chooser' to place them in preference order. Then give them a sticky note to stick in their planner with a **Values for Now** heading. The point is, students should think, talk and debate values and search for what it means to act with integrity.

Activity

Do a brief role play. A customer goes into a shop with three values, in role, of their choice. The values are played by three other students The shopkeeper is distracted for a moment. The customer turns to the 'value' role player and debates whether to take advantage of the shopkeeper's distraction. (This has the feel of a medieval morality play, although don't always make this analogy!) Say this is partly what it means to act with integrity. We are all tempted sometimes, but what sees you through is **integrity. Walking and talking with your values.**

At this school age, students should be allowed to try out different values, to **refine to define**. That is, draft the language, see how the words they choose 'fit' their lives and their thoughts. There is another acronym for this: **FIT**. What **Feel, Imagine and Think,** should be shaped by your values? So, ask: 'Do our values FIT?'

Organize yourself

Many students you will find need this skill. Leaders organize themselves and take a pride in doing so. The best leaders are meticulous in meeting deadlines, turning up on time, getting ready what they need and doing what they say they will. In other words, they have dependability. They acquire a reputation for reliability and personal strength. They are able to decide how the following three aspects need to interrelate:

- Resources
- Aims
- Results.

Develop an ethos of pride. The group would get ready for the workshops by making sure that their uniform is good, that they have what they need. They belong to a prestige team, valued by parents, school and the community. Again and again, it was found that the sense of being a leader brought with it a resonance that could be used. Having students speak at staff meetings, tutor groups, assemblies, council meetings, even at the Houses of Parliament helped their sense of worth. Local MPs are delighted to host tours to the Houses of Parliament. Students often talk for a long time afterwards about being able to speak their mind in the Commons Chamber. Out of session, this is perfectly possible.

Activity

Say to the group: 'Year 7 is having a difficult time starting lessons well. The students are disorganized. They need your help. What could you do?'

Three things emerged from this. Two students gave a talk to the Year 7 assembly about getting prepared the night before for school. They gave practical advice about where to leave your school bag and PE kit so you wouldn't forget them; they did a role play emptying a school bag onto a table, disposing of everything that wasn't essential. They devised an acronym that was used with the year group: **PRP – pen, ruler, planner.** They had the head of Year 7 adopt this with her tutor team as the 'lesson ready routine acronym'. Staff were happy to take it on. Lessons began with teachers saying something like: 'Let's get this lesson right. Let's get the PRP right.'

Activity

Take an exemplary and achievable task such as getting homework done. Split it into three. **Resources: what do you need? Who do you need?** It was found that students didn't know they could use each other as a study group, virtual or at break and lunchtime. **Aims: what do I want to get out of this?** Again, it is possible to say that leaders do things because they know that the long-term benefits will be: deferred gratification. In a workshop situation, the six degrees of separation are used to make a link between any homework and outcome. Group members become each of the 'degrees'. A six-step link from a Geography homework and President of the USA was held. One: you get a good grade in your homework; two: your GCSE is passed; three: you get into post-16 learning of your choice; three: you get a degree; four: you meet someone who sees your potential and offers you a job working for a law firm; five: you get elected as a USA senator because you've excelled at helping people in your law firm; six: you stand for and are elected to the White House. The conversation during the activity defined the learning. There were agreements, questions and revelations as students made the links. 'I didn't know these things were so connected,' someone said. And doing it kinesthetically means you can stop and have a brief role play at the point of a job interview: 'So you got a decent set of grades? You must have done your homework. You've invested in yourself. That time you spent in Year 9 has really paid off.'

Use your ambition to motivate yourself

There's nothing intrinsically wrong with ambition. Use the A of ambition to trigger its definitions and benefits.

Activity

Each person has to think of a definition for or a sentence about ambition, beginning with or containing the letter A. It's surprising how such a simple activity reveals and provokes important ideas. Students say things such as: A for A grade; A for assistance for someone else; A for actual help for people who need it; A for after school, other people who need your success; A for act now so your family will benefit. A means astounding wealth. Wealth? No problem when set in a community context. There are rich conversations to be had about what wealth means: ideas, help, care, medicines and books. The key is to help students see that their ambition is important for people they know. It is also important for people they have yet to meet and those they will never meet.

Essentially, we are selecting those leadership skills that have had the greatest impact. They change from time to time and school to school. That's because the needs of leaders and schools change. Some schools say they need cultural changes for behaviour to improve and design leadership objectives specifically for those changes. Others plan the objectives around the group of students taking the course.

Use these skills as your learning objectives and the students can use them to self and peer assess.

Leadership and learning

In this section context behind the designing learning to lead course and some practice examples for **bringing theory to the classroom** are shared.

Leadership is learning. When students learn well, they lead their own learning. They think about what they need to learn; make decisions about how to learn and who to learn with; think through the resources they need and plan their use; and they self and peer assess. **All these are acts of leadership**. At its best, leading learning involves others: when students co-construct their learning, making resources with each other and using them in self-initiated study sessions.

Following are six practice examples:

Study groups: students form study groups, meeting in their own time, lunchtime, break time, after school, or in the holidays. They plan their study together, mapping out what they will revise over a week or two weeks. They decide what expertise exists within the group, choosing, say, two or three each and leading sessions in their chosen fields.

Target partners: at the start of the lesson, students choose a target partner. They tell this leader to help them self-assess. They choose an aspect or aspects of learning to focus on through the lesson. Then, in periodic mid-lesson plenaries, say: 'Turn to your target partner and lead her through a self-assessment.' Teach her a few leadership questions 'What do you think you've achieved? What do you think you need to do next? What have you made progress (or not made progress) in?' This aspect of encouraging metacognition can build learning capacity.

Learning objective leaders: at the start of the lesson, have a student write up the learning objectives as you explain them. The advantages are many: the students will pay attention to a student writing them up; the student leading this will only write what she understands so it makes you explain it even more carefully; and leaders can be encouraged to write only the keywords of the objective. The class can help by suggesting these. In five minutes, you have engaged the class with the objectives and created a sense of shared ownership.

Learning assessors: appoint two or three learning assessors. These leaders help the peer and self-assessment during mid- and end-lesson plenaries. They can ask the class: 'What have you learned today? What do you need to learn next? When you learned well, what was it that helped you most?'

Learning planners: have three students lead questions around the **what, how** and **you** of learning. The students come to the front of the room. One asks: '**What are you going to learn today? What do you need for your progress?**' The next asks: '**How are you going to learn? Will you try a learning style you don't usually use, like a mind map, or a role play or an annotated list?**' And the third leader says: '**What about your outcome? How will you know whether you've made any progress? What will you do to check the next steps?**' These questions can be on prompt cards, projected on the whiteboard like a teleprompter. Eventually students will think of tweaks to the questions so that they own them and make them specific to the class or even the individual needs of individual students.

Behaviour leaders: have students lead behaviour by setting class targets. These should be highly focused classroom attitudes such as: **starting the lesson by telling the class three aspects of behaviour that they think helped in the previous lesson;**

listening to each other during group work; stopping to listen to the teacher in less than five seconds when an activity changes; reflecting back to the class their assessment of the best behaviour in the room at mid-lesson plenary point or at the end of the lesson; recommending to the head of year the students who have shown courtesy, positive attitudes or cooperation.

Keeping a leading learner log

Having students keep a **learning log** for three weeks at a time helps them to reflect on the ways they learned, the most useful teaching they encountered and what progress they think they have made. This is called a leadership act because they are leading their own learning. They are learning the language and skills of self reflection, organization and evaluation. At a challenge level, students can be encouraged to suggest ways in which they might design their own learning activity. The grid opposite (and on the website) can be used to set the challenge.

Self-initiated learning is being encouraged here. This is leadership: **personal** because students are moving themselves on practically and cognitively. It is also **positive influence over others**, where students choose to design an action that will involve others, stimulate their thinking, have them ask questions and, crucially, make them curious. This latter encourages high-impact learning outcomes. The link between retention and curiosity is strong. A leader of learning creates the possibility for others to wonder, re-evaluate and imagine.

Leader learning log

Show me and I see	Listen and I hear	Do and I understand
How could you design a visual representation of what you need to learn?	How could you make a sound version of what you need to learn?	What could you do with your learning to help others, to make a positive change or influence the attitude of someone else?
Three examples:	**Three examples:**	**Three examples:**
Make a mind map summarizing the keywords and connections between different aspects of today's lesson content.	Make a podcast for your class to hear about what you learned today.	Teach today's lesson to someone else and have him or her feedback to you what he or she has learned.
Design a multi-coloured, connected list with the most important knowledge first.	Invent a rhyme using keywords from the content of your lesson.	Offer to feedback to the class what you think they learned last lesson and predict what might come next.
Break the content up into different-coloured sticky notes and place them where you'll see them every day for a week.	Create a piece of music that reminds you or connects to or represents the content of any lesson.	How could your school be improved as a result of today's lesson? For example, if you learned about recycling, write a letter or article for the school newsletter giving six practical ways other people could make a change in their lives.
What will you design?	What was the outcome?	What change have you noticed in your understanding or in other people?

7 How to use these materials

The following activities can be used in afterschool, pre-school and lunchtime sessions. They can be used in pastoral, citizenship, or personal, health and social education (PHSE) lessons too.

Some schools decide to use this material in curriculum time. It's up to you. Feel free to change and customize these ideas. That's what leaders do: innovate and adapt.

Sometimes a group of students is invited to take the course. There are usually 30 students who take the course for five terms. Invite the students on the recommendation of their head of year, who know which students are likely to benefit from leadership learning. The students are always a comprehensive profile: some have histories of underachievement and low, medium or high levels of classroom disruption. Some have high aspirations and need the structure, language and challenge of leadership learning to keep them on a trajectory to high achievement and very significant progress.

Leadership is for everyone. Having a diverse group of students from a rich range of backgrounds and self-perceptions makes them a fascinating team to develop. Their stories, registers and world views can all be important resources upon which to draw in the activities that make up the course.

Sometimes schools have also used learning to lead as a whole year group programme. In the Warwickshire Local Authority programme I developed, some colleagues wanted the whole of a younger age group cohort to work on the course. In one school, I led this into two year groups. The benefits are significant, especially when working on the group and personal challenges. These can create a real excitement around the school when hundreds of students are leading community improvement projects.

8 Structuring the course

The activities can be followed in any order you wish. They have been grouped into two strands:

- How to lead yourself
- How to lead your community.

You will know your students better than anyone else. You'll see the progression they make through understanding their potential to beginning to apply this with greater confidence and skill. Sometimes you'll need to pause and use strategies and activities you've used before to get back on track. Progression isn't neatly linear in any learning. The activities are a process, not a prescription.

It is important to start with activities and games that encourage **leading yourself**. Then introduce more activities that are about **leading others** and then develop **leadership for the community**.

Realizing potential is a good first step. Students beginning to redefine leadership as something for everyone is key. Slowly they will start to improve their own lives; they will begin to believe they have the skills to make high leverage small changes.

Then they will see how they can **improve others**. This can start with one or two others; then small groups. The leadership group or tutor group provides a safe place to develop these skills. Discussing what went well, what needs improvement in their skills is better done in a small group setting. It can also be done in reflection through a leadership learning log on their e-portfolio. The learning objectives in **'What leadership means'** can be used and encourage students to reflect every half term on their development and what they thought they needed to work on.

Working to change their community is the exciting third phase. It is blended into most of the other earlier activities, but it really starts to have a widespread effect at the personal and group challenge points. If you have a group of 30 or more students following the course and they all take part in a group challenge at the same time, over a short period of, say, six weeks, you can release significant excitement and positive change energy throughout a year group and provoke curiosity and intrigue from other students in the rest of the school.

Certification

Tell students that they will get a certificate at the end. **Say that you will reward their commitment with school recognition. 'We will say you have qualified as a leader.'** What sort of certificate? LAs, local businesses and universities will often help you design and 'badge' such certificates: schools' communities are increasingly aware of the need to build leadership skills for the future and help motivate students in whatever ways they can.

We call it the **Student Leadership Certificate. It has a powerful motivating effect.** As a bespoke certificate, students are able to say they completed a course of learning in leadership and use this in interviews for courses and jobs. It keeps the students focused through the weeks. They report that they feel the learning will have a benefit to their future prospects.

Here's what the students say: 'I'm sure this is going to help me get a job. People want leaders.' 'All the employers and people from the university told us that leadership skills are in demand these days.' 'You need all the help you can get to get employed.' 'Learning to lead gave me more confidence. It helped me think through situations where I could make change happen. It helped me build teams to get things done. It made me better at being assertive and not bossy.' 'Speaking in front of teachers, parents, local councillors, even MPs made me realize how much worth I have and the skills I have at explaining and persuading.' 'Learning to lead is about understanding yourself and other people. It changed my view of what a leader is. It's about change, sometimes big, sometimes small.' 'I didn't know I could be a leader at the start. Now I know I can.' 'I don't have to let life just happen to me. I can make a difference.'

Spreading the learning over five terms and having periodic assessment every term enhances the focus and the status of the work. Students feel that they are part of a high value process.

Learning leadership can contribute to other external accreditation such as: **Wider Key Skills Certification; Award Scheme Development and Accreditation Network (ASDAN); functional skills literacy.**

Using the leadership skill grid

Each activity has a range of connected learning objectives. These are ticked in the grid. The intention is that you should adapt this grid to suit yourself.

If these leadership skills do not suit your context, invent new ones, possibly with your students and their community.

Positive influence over others	**Positive influence over yourself**		
	Using your personal integrity	Organize yourself	Use your ambition to motivate yourself
Give instructions to help a group task			
Guide other people			
Question to secure a task objective			
Set an example			
Take a longer-term view of things			
Take the initiative			
Show courage and determination			
Inspire the trust of others			
Empathize with others			
Organize others			

Natali – Student voice

We discussed these skills with a year head and a member of our business community. We asked them what leadership skills they thought we ought to develop, which were going to be important in the future.

Some of us kept a leadership log grid. We scored our skills as we went along. Each month we would ask a partner to give us a score for each skill and we would self-assess. This was extra easy because we kept our work on the computer in our own e-leadership folder.

Functional skills

The materials are an ideal way to prepare for the functional skill assessments in speaking and listening. Each of the activities is linked to a **functional skill speaking and listening criteria at level 2**. So, as well as improving the leadership abilities of your students, you can prepare them for three compulsory accreditations. It gives an extra edge to the learning: students feel they are getting something for it that they need at GCSE and post-16 success. KS2 students can feel they are preparing for GCSE level qualifications as early as Year 6.

A possible timescale for a leadership course

If you want to plan a leadership course lasting five terms as an out-of-school activity, it might look something like the one opposite (also available on the website).

A five-term leadership course

Term 1 (spring)	Term 2 (summer)	Term 3 (autumn Year 9)
Launch		
After school workshops 1, 2 and 3	After school workshops 4 and 5	After school workshops 6 and 7
2 lunchtime meetings	2 lunchtime meetings	2 lunchtime meetings
Assessment sheet	Prepare personal challenge	Assess personal challenge. Affirmations
• Parental letters sent home • Staff support: tutors reinforcing the benefits • Business support: visitors being interviewed, being part of the end of term celebration	• Second term self-assessment • Parents invited in to be part of the celebration and term 2 certificate award ceremony	• Parental letters home • A guest from the community, local mayor, MP or councillor giving the students a sense of self worth and confidence

Term 4 (spring Year 9)	Term 5 (summer Year 9)
After school workshops 8 and 9	After school workshop 10
2 lunchtime meetings	1 lunchtime meeting
Prepare group challenge	Assess group challenge
• Parental letters • Business support • Staff meeting presentation • Tutors invited to a workshop to celebrate students getting this far • Community representatives. The author used alumni who each had a story to tell, bringing up a family, working in the health service, running their own business. Students sensed they were going to join a group of successful people in their own fields. Again, challenge students to re-think what a leader is. Work with them every day. They change and shape our lives. Often the best leaders are those who we do not notice	GRADUATION. Invite parents, community leaders, and university and business leaders. The author held this at a local university and in school. Create an occasion of significant achievement. Public celebration of students who thought this was beyond them is so important

Of course, the time you take depends on the needs you have. **Spacing the programme out over five terms means there is less demand on the time of the students and staff and more of a slow incremental build up of skills.**

This time span also develops a sense of commitment to the programme from the students and allows them to build a feeling that they are part of a team getting to know each other and building trust.

Other schools have built the programme into their PHSE learning. Some weave the activities into existing schemes of work so that one lesson a fortnight is explicitly about leadership.

Some schools devote a whole term to ten sessions of leadership learning, mixing after-school with timetabled lessons.

The mix that is right for you will depend on the needs of your students and the structures of your school. What we have all found in common is that teaching leadership explicitly gives students a sense that they have important life skills, valued by others and important to their school and life chances.

9   Self-assessment

Using assessment to help you improve your leadership skills

Improvement is a team business. Everyone is here to lead your change. The other members of the group, the staff, your family, they all want to help you become a leader. So, think small steps. Think how you could support others and what support you need for those around you.

Positive influence over others	**Positive influence over yourself**		
	Using your personal integrity	Organize yourself	Use your ambition to motivate yourself
Give instructions to help a group task	✔		
Guide other people			
Question to secure a task objective			
Set an example			
Take a longer-term view of things			
Take the initiative			
Show courage and determination			
Inspire the trust of others			
Empathize with others			
Organize others			

Time needed: 20 minutes

How to

Every term, have the students self-assess. There is a range of purposes:

- To help students learn how to **choose assessment criteria** and thus have some ownership over self-assessment.
- To help students think through **who would make an effective assessor**: this helps build trust in the assessment process and again places an element of control in the leader's hands.
- It provides an opportunity for students and others to **see progression**.

Set great store by this. At the end of each term have a '**graduation**'. If students have made acceptable progress, they graduate to the next term. Parents and other interested staff attend and celebrate what's been achieved.

Use the **leadership self-assessment sheet** (see online resources). Students choose four other lessons outside of English, maths and ICT. They then choose three other areas not to do with school. Students are free to choose learning to lead workshops as one area. This has many advantages and proves quite popular, leading to an increased level of mutual co-support. Students say to each other, they need high grades and can they be given a high profile role in the workshops to show off their abilities.

They choose two of the 13 objectives. Then they take the assessment sheet to the assessors. For the lessons, these are the teachers, but for, say, improvement in their sports team, this might be a team member; for home leadership, this could be a parent or carer. This latter is so powerful, especially when the parents then attend the graduation and see the outcomes of their input.

It's important to stress that the baseline scores should be low and not to worry about that. Say: 'You are here to learn. You have the potential and you will improve these scores.' It is better that the assessors are straight, even if this means giving a low score. The sense of accomplishment at the end of term when they see scores rising make this worthwhile.

Again, it's worth spending a little time modelling how to ask for scores from staff; this can be done with a volunteer student and the co-teacher in the group. Talk about how to ask, and what to say when the score is added, especially if it is low. Work at the level of thanking staff whatever the score; how to mask what they really feel and how to self talk the determination to improve.

Challenge

Invite students to attend a staff briefing to let colleagues know what they are doing in their self-assessment. Not all the students will want to speak. But, for those who do, this is important. They need preparation and rehearsal, and the staff can be invited to respond and welcome students in any way appropriate to the setting. It works well when the students go into the briefing, which can be held in the hall, with applause from the staff. They sit in a line at the front and two students show on the projector the assessment sheets they will be using over the next three weeks. Then they briefly explain how these work. They then describe how they will be going to staff for scores. Another leader is briefed to explain how staff could score, what the four-point scale means.

This is an important session. It lasts only ten minutes but has a lasting effect on students. They repeat this sort of staff presentation several times over the course of the five terms, sometimes to report back on learning styles they felt to be working, sometimes with suggestions for operational improvements in the school's running, and at the end for congratulations when they have graduated.

Aadarsh – Student voice

It helped to talk through what to say if you got a low score to start with. It's hard to take if you disagree with it. But you have to accept this is how you have come across. And you have to fix it. We tried to talk through how to support each other if this happened. We talked about low scores we'd got, why it might be and what we could do to get the scores higher. There was a real sense of team spirit. If someone was in difficulty, we helped.

Discussion points

- How can we help each other achieve higher scores? What can we practically do in the classroom to help?
- How do you feel when you got a low score? How can you turn this feeling into determination? Visualize something you want to achieve; see yourself being someone you admire; see the change you need to make. Keep the change small; break it down into something you can do in the next hour, the next day, the next week.
- **RACE your change** (see below). Find a target partner. Have him or her coach your improvement. Check back with the teacher or team member who gave you the low score. Ask, with courtesy, 'How am I doing? What do I need to do next?'

Leadership tip

The assessment sheets can be used twice a term: once to get a baseline and once, three or four weeks later, to gauge improvements. Set targets personal to the students, with them for ownership. Do this once they've got their first set of baselines. These are called **RACE targets**: Realistic, Agreed, Challenging for Excellence.

Depending on the group, you can 'edge the bar higher' and say, 'If you don't meet your target, you can't graduate the term.' Then give, say, a fortnight to improve the score in specific areas. Most students respond to the challenge and self-competition this creates.

Part 2

50 Leadership Activities

How to Lead Yourself

Activity 1: If it's to be – it's up to me

Helping someone else is a key leadership role. Thinking to yourself, 'Who can I help and how can I do this?' is central to becoming a leader.

Positive influence over others	Positive influence over yourself		
	Using your personal integrity	Organize yourself	Use your ambition to motivate yourself
Give instructions to help a group task	✔		✔
Guide other people			
Question to secure a task objective			
Set an example			
Take a longer-term view of things			
Take the initiative	✔		✔
Show courage and determination			
Inspire the trust of others			
Empathize with others	✔	✔	
Organize others			

Time needed: 20 minutes

How to

This requires the teacher to take on a role. The teacher takes on a low status role as a new person in the school. You have been introduced to the group and you are a little unsure of yourself. You are uncertain about the way you look, the way you dress. You don't feel confident.

Ask the students to pair up and think of appropriate ways to respond.

Then, as a whole group, the students give their advice and counsel.

Make this as easy or difficult as you like. Make it difficult for the leaders to make you feel positive, so that they have to regroup and think through new strategies and advice.

Give students the following content: 'You move towards and become like what you think about.'

Tell them that this can be proven when they are riding a bike: if you look at something while you ride along, you'll find yourself unconsciously steering towards it. This is why it's so important to keep your eyes on where you want to go in order to keep safe and healthy.

This is a key part of the course content. Learning that your thoughts dictate your actions, self-belief and motivation are key to self-change and leadership growth.

Additional idea

Ask students what they want to believe about themselves and to anonymously write it on a sticky note. Feed them back, but do not treat them as a guessing game as to who wrote each one. Keep reminding students that the more they think these positive thoughts and ideas, the more they will move towards them. This all prepares students for a later activity: 'Writing and living affirmations'.

Natali – Student voice

I do think badly of myself too often. When I stopped to think about it, most of my thoughts are sort of negative. So I really tried hard, three times a day to think a positive thought and it worked. I tried saying it out loud and that worked so long as I explained what I was doing!

Discussion points

- What can we say to someone to reassure them that appearance doesn't really matter?
- How can we help people to understand that everyone now feels the same?
- What can a leader do to help others see that really we all have the same worries and insecurities?

Leader tip

The teacher in role input helps students to see that it isn't just young people who worry about everyday things. Their suggestions, thoughts and even role play solutions give them confidence that they have leadership abilities. When you are in role, you can thank them for their thoughts. You can tell them how much of what they've said has helped.

Activity 2: Define me

This game will help students come to a definition of themselves and help them see that this is under their own control.

Positive influence over others	Positive influence over yourself		
	Using your personal integrity	Organize yourself	Use your ambition to motivate yourself
Give instructions to help a group task			
Guide other people			
Question to secure a task objective			
Set an example			✔
Take a longer-term view of things		✔	
Take the initiative			
Show courage and determination		✔	
Inspire the trust of others		✔	
Empathize with others			
Organize others			

Time needed: 20 minutes

How to

Ask the group to think of ten 'emotion' words each. Put these on sticky notes around the room. It can be helpful to list ten or so on the display to get them started: kind, thoughtful, helpful, confident, shy. Then have the group collect three that they think apply to them.

Plenary: ask the group to pair up and discuss which of the emotions they are proud of and which they would like to change. Say: your plenary partner may have a suggestion for you to help change the emotion you don't want.

Suggest an emotion swap. Say: your plenary partner may want to change an emotion with you. If he or she does, talk about when you feel this emotion. What helps you? Talk about times when you've felt this and what's encouraged you.

Now pair with someone else and do the same. Tell him or her what you started with and what you swapped. You may swap again and again, explain why you want the emotion you've swapped. Your partner may have a suggestion to help you lead into this emotion.

Say: if you've got an emotion you swapped, **you defined yourself.** This is what leaders do. They choose what they want to feel.

Next: role play. In pairs, play a right and wrong reaction. Your teacher says you haven't done your homework. But you think you have. You have genuinely forgotten it. You have a hard time persuading your teacher. In role play 1, show the group how to get it wrong. Then show the same scene but define yourself. Show us how to choose emotions that will help you show your leadership skills.

This leads on to a discussion about leadership emotions in this situation such as: dignity, restraint, calm. When you show these role plays, have students choose emotions from the sticky notes on the wall and offer them to the in role student to see if they work. Students get intrigued when they are offered four or five emotions on the sticky notes: the key is saying: 'You've got a group of emotions to choose from. Which will you choose? Which would show you as a leader?' Make the point that this is what leaders do, they have a 'store' of emotions in their repertoire from which they can select, not just leap to the first one that comes along.

Challenge

In groups of three, students write one emotion they best think defines a leader. Again, a displayed vocabulary helps the students' leadership register. They write their one word on a sheet of A3 so it can be seen from a distance.

Attach these to the far side of the classroom and have the class stand at the other end. Then say to the students: 'Choose the emotion you find most attractive at this moment, today, now. When I tell you, move slowly towards it.' Give them thinking time. Then they make what is called a 'leadership walk', that is, they walk towards an emotion word they are attracted to. Emphasize that leaders consciously 'walk towards', choose, the emotions they most need to accomplish a task or goal. They will inevitably end up with more than two or three with each emotion.

Power talk: say to the class 'You have five minutes to talk with each other about your chosen words. Ask why they want this feeling? Ask why it would help? In which situations would it be useful? Ask each other what you could do to grow more in this direction. Think of something practical you could try to help gain this emotion: today and in the next few days.

Power talk: a term for highly focused time deadlined student chaired discussion. It should take five minutes. Emphasize no wasted time. Get a feedback at the end about the quality of focused, on-task talk. It seems to be the phase power talk that makes a slight but important difference to the focus when you've only got 15–20 minutes to introduce the activity, its purpose and reflect on the quality of the outcome.

Tatyana – Student voice

I like the idea that you can change things in yourself and others. There's nothing more important than having the courage to look at your own feelings and see how they can be controlled.

Discussion points

- How possible is it to choose what you feel?
- How much can you choose who you want to be?
- How can others help you lead towards the emotions you need?

Leadership tip

Pace is important: that's why there are things such as 'power talk'. It gives an edge to reflection. We still insist on thoughtful reflection. But, as in the next exercise, letting students see that their talk and thought have the power to make small and important changes is a strong incentive to reflect.

Activity 3: Power thinking

Good leaders are power thinkers. This game will help students' thinking potential.

Positive influence over others	Positive influence over yourself		
	Using your personal integrity	Organize yourself	Use your ambition to motivate yourself
Give instructions to help a group task			
Guide other people	✔		
Question to secure a task objective		✔	
Set an example			
Take a longer-term view of things			✔
Take the initiative			
Show courage and determination		✔	
Inspire the trust of others			
Empathize with others	✔		
Organize others		✔	

Time needed: 30 minutes

How to

Have you ever thought you couldn't do something or you aren't capable of accomplishing a goal? It's a common feeling. Most of our lives we are expected to put up with second best or be told by someone that success isn't cool. Leadership steers you away from this. And, even more powerfully, you can help other people to take control of their thinking too.

The group of students stands in a line facing you. Take an everyday task or activity such as completing your maths homework. Tell the members of the group that they are a 'Thought Spectrum'. At one end is negative thinking. At the other end is positive thinking.

Now have the negative end start with the most negative thought they can think of about maths homework. This will be something such as, 'I can't do it'. Now introduce the group to what a leader does. A leader will try to be as positive as he or she can, while still being realistic; stress that making small changes can be powerful. Here, for instance, say: 'Tell youself "I can't do my maths homework yet".' It's a small change but important because it leaves the door open to positive change. Students nudge their thinking to the positive. The person next in line takes the thought and makes it slightly more positive. This might become, 'I don't think I can do it'. The important thing about this game is to imagine slight improvements as the students go down the line. That's where some of the key learning takes place: learning how to take a thought and incrementally change it.

Too often in life we hear people say, 'Pull yourself together,' or 'Buck up your ideas'. Life doesn't work like this and a leader recognizes this. Make many slight improvements and they all add up to help improve things.

Sometimes the students' comments go backwards. And this will come out in this game. As the thought line gets ever more positive, students will say something that seems to take the flow back to the negative. Tell them: 'This is normal; this is what happens in real life. Life isn't a perfect flow from feeling down to feeling wonderful.' What's important for them is to see how non-linear the process can be.

You will be amazed at how the thought changes. By the time you have reached the end of the line, students will be saying things such as, 'This homework is the best thing that's ever happened to me, I can't wait to ask for more!'Of course, they'll say this to be funny. But accept this. It is a game after all. Then talk about how you become like and move towards what you think about. Students may well resist the idea that you can change your thoughts consciously. This is important to challenge. This is part of their prior expectation.

Challenge

Have students write down in their homework planner two positive thoughts in two spaces where they expect homework that week. Discuss what they are going to write in pairs. Tell them: 'Think of the spectrum we just played, has your partner thought of a way to nudge your thinking even more positively? You'll know when it's gone too far. It'll be something you sense.' Use the notion of the comfort zone. You want students to move into what we call 'comfort zone plus' or just outside it, but not so far that it becomes demotivating.

Aadarsh – Student voice

It did feel strange to be taking a thought and changing it to be more positive bit by bit. We got it wrong lots of times and it wouldn't get more positive till we helped each other and changed it. That's the point of this game. You improve each other's thoughts. That's what a leader does.

Discussion points
- What do you do when you face difficulty?
- How can you change your thought slightly?
- Think of a time when you've felt challenged by something or somebody.
- What helped you overcome it? Tell the group about such a time. Discuss the ways you built your own self-esteem.

Leadership tip

You can refer to the Thought Spectrum at any time the group encounters a difficulty with something facing them in or out of school. It also works in groups of four or five. It's even easier for students to think of a slightly more positive change when the numbers are small.

You can say to the group, 'We all have a Thought Spectrum inside us. We can move up or down the scale whenever we want. It will be difficult at first but become easier with time and talk. The game we have just done will help you to visualize this and remember it.'

Activity 4: Positive and negative charge game

Students will think about how they are someone else's responsibility and how it is a leader's job to look out for others even when he or she doesn't know what's happening.

Positive influence over others	Positive influence over yourself		
	Using your personal integrity	Organize yourself	Use your ambition to motivate yourself
Give instructions to help a group task		✔	
Guide other people			
Question to secure a task objective			✔
Set an example			
Take a longer-term view of things	✔		
Take the initiative			
Show courage and determination			
Inspire the trust of others			
Empathize with others		✔	
Organize others	✔		

Time needed: 20 minutes

How to

Discuss with the students who they feel responsible for. Do they have to organize anyone or look after anyone? What skills and advice do they have that could be passed on?

This game will help students to think about how a leader is responsible for someone in everyday life, even people they don't know and who don't know them. A large, empty space is required in order to play it.

To play, first choose someone in the room who will be the 'positive charge'. Next choose someone who is the 'negative charge'. Choose at random but do not let anyone know who you have chosen. There must be no particular reason for your choice.

To begin the game, say to the students: 'Start moving around the space. You must keep your positive charge between you and your negative charge at all times. Use the 'positive charge' person as a 'secret shield'. Don't let either your positive charge or negative charge know you have chosen them. Look out for them. Watch out for where they are. Keep moving but don't make it obvious what you are avoiding and who is your secret shield. Have fun! If you accidentally end up colliding with your negative charge, they have won!'

Additional idea

Tell your negative and positive charges that you will be taking responsibility for giving them some positive encouragement over the next two days. You will be looking out for them and giving them feedback on anything you notice they do well.

Michael – Student voice

I found it challenging to look out for someone I didn't really know. But it's important. It would be really good if everyone did this, if you came to school and thought, people I don't even know want me to do well and think I'm good at something.

Discussion points

- How far can you go to take responsibility for someone?
- What would it be like if you knew how many people wanted you to do well?
- How could this happen in schools? When would you get good feedback from someone?
- How can this be done without it being embarrassing or patronizing?

Leader tip

Model how to give positive feedback. Role play with a volunteer how to keep your voice sincere, or what to write in his or her planner, or what to tell another teacher about.

Activity 5: Fall trust

'I'll be there when you fall.' We all need someone to catch us. A leader has a key role helping everyone realize this.

Positive influence over others	Positive influence over yourself		
	Using your personal integrity	Organize yourself	Use your ambition to motivate yourself
Give instructions to help a group task	✔		
Guide other people			
Question to secure a task objective			
Set an example	✔	✔	
Take a longer-term view of things			
Take the initiative	✔	✔	
Show courage and determination			
Inspire the trust of others	✔	✔	✔
Empathize with others	✔	✔	
Organize others	✔	✔	

Time needed: 20 minutes

How to

This is a simple trust game. It's a good one with which to start a session. 'A, you will help and sustain B. A stand about two feet behind B. B, when you feel **trust and are secure** and when you hear a **confident, assertive invitation**, gently fall back. A will catch you by putting their arms under yours. He will stop you falling and then help you return to your original position.' Before you start, you can ask the group what they think they'll need to do this well. Refer to the learning objectives in the table. Afterwards, ask the partners to feedback to each other. How safe did they feel? Was there anything they could have said to make the leadership more confident or more deserving of trust? Straightforward skills are required:

a calm voice, using the name of the person falling and being clear about the cue for falling. This is better as a request followed by 'thank you'.

Challenge

If the partners are evenly matched physically, they can fall towards each other. The falling student can even try closing his or her eyes when falling. If it helps, have two people catch. They place their hands on the shoulders of the person falling and gently return them to a standing position. Another variant is falling forward and backward: this can be done without the catchers letting go of the shoulders of the faller. If they stand close enough, the falling has more of a sense of rocking back and forth. Relaxing music helps. It's a good bonding game. The leadership talk is about safety, empathy and care.

Use the 'thought box' for everyone to write the names of up to three people who have caught them in the past. Then pull these out, anonymously. Tell students beforehand what you will be doing and that this isn't a game to guess the names of these people. Most students will want to tell the group that they wrote the names being read out. Let them explain, if they wish, why they wrote those names and why they felt 'caught' by those and individuals and how they had been supported. The individuals they've written down all have leadership qualities so, at this point, everyone is learning from them.

Michael – Student voice

I liked being able to talk about how helpful my mum and dad have been to me. They make me feel confident. They catch me when I need it. They seem to know when I need help. Sometimes they know this before I do. My best friends are like this too.

The game made me think. What if we all knew we were looking out for each other? I think that would make us feel stronger, able to work harder, to try harder knowing if we didn't get a lesson, say, someone would be watching out and ready to help if they could.

Discussion points

- In life, what kind of events mean we need catching? How can a leader help?
- How do we help people around us to **rely on us but not be dependent?**
- What is the difference between being **dependent and interdependent?**

Leader tip

The game is powerful as a metaphor for what leaders do to give reassurance. We want our leaders to give a sense that they will be supportive, and on the look out for when others need 'catching' – usually these are about temporary states of loneliness, or stress and anxiety, say at test and exam times. The skill of the leader lies in spotting the moment someone needs support and providing it in the right way. What if we had schools where everyone felt supported by a network of leaders? What if that network became the critical mass? What if everyone felt they had that potential or even that responsibility?

Activity 6: Blind trust

This game will help students to develop the trust of others in their leadership

Positive influence over others	Positive influence over yourself		
	Using your personal integrity	Organize yourself	Use your ambition to motivate yourself
Give instructions to help a group task	✔		
Guide other people			
Question to secure a task objective			
Set an example	✔	✔	
Take a longer-term view of things			
Take the initiative	✔	✔	
Show courage and determination	✔	✔	✔
Inspire the trust of others	✔	✔	✔
Empathize with others	✔	✔	
Organize others	✔	✔	

Time needed: 30 minutes

How to

Say to students, 'This will help you to think about trust, what it means, how to gain it and how to keep it.' Have the students pair up: A and B. Row A stands in a line at one end of the room. Row B stands in a line at the other end. 'Directly face your partner. B, tell your partner that you can trust them.' Use the **leadership language display**: have someone on the laptop scribing a couple of useful phrases which you can co-construct: 'Don't worry', is fine, but get them to make the language positive. 'You can trust me. I will look after you. I will lead you well.' It's about making this language routine and bringing it into their comfort zone.

Then set a few obstacles between the two lines: tables, chairs and so on. When you start the game, have A close their eyes and B guide them, without contact, around the obstacles. They must not make contact with anything or anyone. They give instructions and requests. Do a power plenary (three minutes to think of three things you have learned or questions about learning and leadership): 'Open your eyes, what leadership phrases are we using to get our partners across?' Generically, the best will be brief, clear and assertive. It is so important to keep refreshing the idea of assertiveness throughout the course. When it routinely means direct, helpful, encouraging and supportive, and not 'bossy', then we are making progress.

Then they continue on their journey. Stress it isn't a race. It's about care and, critically, empathy. They need to understand the concept that for this to work, they have to imagine what it's like to be someone else.

Challenge

Ask students the differences between 'looking' and 'seeing'. This isn't a value judgement, but it's important to get them thinking about it. For the author, looking means observing, standing back, and being as objective as you can; it also means being curious, wondering, asking questions about what appears to be happening, in any situation. Seeing is about beginning to understand the reasons for what you find; forming a hypothesis; asking yourself what you could do, how you could lead. Stress that looking and seeing are key elements of leadership.

Discuss the differences between empathy and sympathy. Hold a 'Chair Spectrum'. Sympathy at one end; empathy at the other. Model or have a student demonstrate how you move from sympathy to empathy. The author defined the difference as: sympathy you know what someone else feels; empathy, you feel what they are going through with them. Sympathy, you face someone and listen; empathy, you are alongside someone and go through the same experiences as them.

Andy – Student voice

It was strange keeping your eyes shut and not colliding with things. We really enjoyed it and wanted to keep playing it. It made us think about why we trusted someone. When we changed partners we could see people's different leadership styles. We took care not to make someone feel less good but it made us realize that different styles are right for different people. Some people prefer a jokey style; some people thought that was distracting. All of us agreed that being told, 'well done, you've got past a really tricky bit, you're doing OK', was helpful, without going over the top. No one likes false praise.

Discussion points

- Why is trust important in leadership?
- Think of a time when you trusted someone and it paid off – or didn't. Discuss with a partner such a time and explore the reasons for it.
- In a lesson, when might it be important for other students and the teacher to trust you? Students usually think of potentially risky physical events such as sports or drama; but with deeper thinking you can get them to levels of thinking around: positive attitudes, modelling optimism for others, helping them with their academic and personal improvement.
- What does empathy mean? Why is it important in leadership? Think of a situation when someone did or didn't empathize with you.

Leadership tip

This game draws on leadership skills on so many levels. Empathy is at its core. We found asking students to think for the following session of events during the week that might have been helped through empathy. Asking students to reflect on everyday situations makes them apply the learning in the workshop. You can take this further by requiring a written or recorded log of thee events. Reflection on action is a key leadership skill for life.

Activity 7: The chair trust game

This exercise will help students think about some of the key skills needed to be a good leader.

	Positive influence over others	Positive influence over yourself	
	Using your personal integrity	Organize yourself	Use your ambition to motivate yourself
Give instructions to help a group task			
Guide other people		✔	
Question to secure a task objective	✔	✔	✔
Set an example			✔
Take a longer-term view of things			✔
Take the initiative			✔
Show courage and determination			✔
Inspire the trust of others	✔		✔
Empathize with others	✔		
Organize others	✔	✔	✔

Time needed: 30 minutes

How to

Say to the leaders: 'I need you to think as you play this trust game. What leadership skills do you think you need for it to work – and be safe?' It may be helpful to display some key vocabulary on the screen during the exercise; for example: trust, confidence, inspire, care, empathy, organize.

Demonstrate first. Emphasize that the leader must help everyone feel safe, trusted and inspire trust in him- or herself. Say: 'There are many ways of doing this. The way you talk to someone. The way you stand in relation to them. The way you look at them. The details of what you say are important, such as using their name, giving an instruction using the phrase "thank you", as well as "please". Sometimes please can sound as though you are pleading. It isn't always appropriate. Thanking someone for doing something in advance makes it sound as though you expect they will do what you need.'Show the students, with a volunteer, how to play. Place a chair about a centimetre behind your standing volunteer. The chair must not make contact with your volunteer. 'The person has no idea whether or not the chair is behind her. She has only got my word for it. Now I am going to invite her to sit. Watch how I do this and give me some feedback on how well I inspire trust.' Of course, this is about offering a chance for reflection, thinking and analysis but it also builds tension.

Now invite the person to sit. Stand directly opposite her stand at 45 degrees to her. Ask which feels more comfortable. Use the person's name. Say: 'I want you to know that you are perfectly safe. I will not let anything harmful happen to you. Do not sit down until I invite you. Try not to reach out with your hands or look around but sit straight down. I assure you there is a chair in place. Are you happy?' Pause. Ask the person and the group to comment on the detail of what you've said and how you said it. Leaders will be sensitive to your tone of voice, your standing position, eye contact, and whether and how you smiled: all these paralinguistic and linguistic features are so important.

Challenge

Say: 'Try sitting down with your eyes closed. Only do this if you feel totally safe and well led.' Of course, you must check that everyone is safe; circulate well, making sure the gaps between the chair and the person sitting are no more than a centimetre.

Natali – Student voice

It felt amazing to do this. It sounded really simple, just to sit down. But when you have no evidence the chair is there and you have to totally trust the leadership of your partner, it makes you really think about leadership. I talked to my partner about how she made me feel secure. And I hadn't thought that leadership was about that. It also made me feel challenged. So that must be what leadership is about too. Feeling safe enough to do something you didn't know you could do.

Discussion points

- When you sat down, what helped you to feel safe? Name three ways you were well led and feed them back to your leader.
- How could you have been even better led?

Leadership tip

Part of the work training leaders is adding to their leadership register. There is a strong literacy strand through this work. We think that the more literate leaders become, the more competent they are at the generic skills of self reflection, analysis and evaluation.

The body language, eye contact and voice tone skills are worth spending time on. Students enjoy experimenting with these and directing you to try a range of styles. It works particularly well if you have a volunteer co-teacher. Of course, the way they direct you can be reflected on. This is a leadership act, to talk and address you in such a way that you feel led rather than pushed into trying alternative tactics.

The following exercise can be used as a starter into some activities. Say: 'Rank order or omit these words from a list of leadership verbs: impel, urge, goad, force, make, induce, exhort, persuade, press, restrain.' It's a short but important activity that can also be done with other lists. Another one found to provoke good quality discussion is: 'guide, show the way, direct, pilot, go in front, go ahead, front, head, conduct, follow, be in charge of, run, control, command, manage.'

Activity 8: Ambition box

Leaders need to think about their ambitions: and how to realize them; how to help each other achieve their goals. This strategy ensures everyone gets to think about these issues in a secure easy process.

Positive influence over others	**Positive influence over yourself**		
	Using your personal integrity	Organize yourself	Use your ambition to motivate yourself
Give instructions to help a group task			
Guide other people		✔	
Question to secure a task objective	✔	✔	✔
Set an example			✔
Take a longer-term view of things			✔
Take the initiative			✔
Show courage and determination			✔
Inspire the trust of others	✔		✔
Empathize with others	✔		✔
Organize others	✔	✔	✔

Time needed: 10/15 minutes

How to

Introduce the activity with a list of the types of predictions futurologists are making for the next ten years. These are readily available. Use a resource such as http://uk.Encarta.msn.Com/encnet/Features/Lists/?article=FuturePredictions. This describes the kind of possible futures for the next ten years. Then discuss the types of jobs this will require.

Ask students to think about what they would most like to do in the next five or ten years. This activity also works with shorter timescales, even as close as this afternoon and tomorrow.

On their own, the students write the future down on a slip of paper and these are collected in a secret box. Tell the students that these will be shared with the group but their names will not be disclosed and this isn't a guessing game. They can acknowledge authorship if they wish.

The group leader takes these one by one and reads them. They are placed, on a prepared display board or transcribed to a laptop through to a data projected display.

Additional idea

Students take two ambitions each and in pairs give advice on the next two or three practical steps to be taken. This can be presented as a 'WWW' grid as shown below.

W	Why do you really want to do this?	
W	What help or skills do you need?	
W	Who do you need to network with?	

This allows students the chance to discuss the principle of collaboration in leadership and how networking enables them to add to their leadership capacity.

Aadarsh – Student voice

We role played a network with some of us as parents, some as teachers, some as university lecturers and some as employers who might help. Then I went from person to person and asked: 'How can you help me?' The answers made me think that it's up to me to make connections between people. This is a positive act. It's about taking responsibility.

This really helped us say things about our futures. We could do it without having to say anything out loud. I wouldn't have minded doing that but I know others did. We don't talk about what we're going to do all the time, not at break and lunchtime anyway. It was really surprising to hear what people were going to do. Some people said more about why they wanted to be a vet or a business person. I thought it might all be about money but it wasn't.

Discussion points

- How in control of your future are you?
- How in control do you want to be?
- Have students lead this part of the discussion. Appoint a chairperson to run a talk queue or snowball this from pairs to fours. Keep a tight time limit.

Leadership tip

It helps if students are absolutely sure they won't be identified. Try playing music to enhance the drama of the event: TV theme tunes work well. Once again, giving students choice over the music to be played is helpful. Having managers for all the jobs linked to activities is essential: giving out the slips, passing the box around, timing, CD player. It might not seem important to have the process tasks delegated but it produces a sense of collective effort.

Activity 9: The ambitions continuum

Invite the students to be open about how ambitious they are for themselves and for others. Leadership is about them and the world around them. This exercise will help them to think about what leadership is for.

	Positive influence over others	**Positive influence over yourself**	
	Using your personal integrity	Organize yourself	Use your ambition to motivate yourself
Give instructions to help a group task			
Guide other people	✔		
Question to secure a task objective			
Set an example	✔		
Take a longer-term view of things		✔	
Take the initiative			
Show courage and determination			✔
Inspire the trust of others	✔	✔	
Empathize with others	✔		
Organize others	✔		

Time needed: 20 minutes

How to

Form an ambitions continuum is a straight line facing the group. On the left is the **superambitious point.** Say: 'You stand here if you live and breath a particular ambition. If you wake up thinking about being a doctor, nurse, lawyer or whatever.' On the right is the **open door point. '**You have no real idea what drives you. You couldn't explain it to anyone. You have a sense of open door. This means, you have a very open mind as to what you might want to be and the person you might want to become.'Say: 'Choose a point on the continuum. Pick the place first in your mind. Once you've chosen it, don't be swayed by seeing where others stand. And, if someone stands where you wanted, just stand directly behind him.' Students can move in twos and threes or all at once.

Then invite students to think about what they see. It's different every time and difficult to predict. Have the line become a circle so the opposite ends meet. Now explore these differences. Without any pressure, simply ask the students to discuss what they were thinking when they chose their standing point. They learn from hearing different perspectives. Insist that no value judgements are made.

Then we make a continuum for a community context. This can be: the group, the school, the local town or village. It's a new thought for many, that's worth reinforcing.

Take the town or village. The **superambitious point** represents how they feel about the place they live in. What do they think it could become? Do they feel any sense of commitment to it? Superambitious shows high levels of commitment. They want a great deal for the fabric and people of where they live. The **open door point** suggests they've never been outside of their family or friendship group, or they don't see it as their responsibility to take part in positive change.

Then 'circle' the line. Debate the differences. This needs obviously sensitive handling. Occasionally difficult local issues can emerge. But as potential leaders they need to tackle these in a supportive setting. Often there's a real sense that 'it's not my job to clean the place up, or protect it from vandalism and graffiti'. We don't expect instant change to views like this. We are asking leaders to think and to meet different perspectives. The line becoming a circle technique helps this to happen.

Challenge

Invite students to challenge their tutor group to do the same activity. What role does the tutor group want to play in improving each other's lives and the learning of the school? One valuable outcome can be that the teacher asks what the activity is, how to do it and what might be learned through doing so. It makes the leaders responsible to helping the teacher, for suggesting an activity.

Michael – Student voice

We really thought about who we could be ambitious for. It made me realize there's more than just me and my friends. It is difficult to think beyond that. But it's important because even in small ways, we can help to lead others we don't know. Even just thinking about what's happening in our town and school is a start. Some people don't even do that.

Discussion points

- What things could you change in your tutor room, in your home room, in your planner?
- Should we start small? Does this stop us aiming high? Or might it help us? Discuss with the group how taking things slowly and in small steps can add up to significant change. It could be helpful to advise the leaders that this is key. What a leader does is to offer realistic ways into hope. Not false hope.
- What is the difference between ambition and aspiration? It matters because we want people around us to be both. The author came to the conclusion that aspiration was 'beyond' ambition.

Leadership tip

The challenge level is especially important. The students having the initiative to suggest learning with the teacher is right at the heart of this course. Co-constructed learning is what so much of this is about.

Activity 10: Ambition still picture

This exercise will help students to deepen their thinking about what they want to do with their leadership potential.

Positive influence over others	Positive influence over yourself		
	Using your personal integrity	Organize yourself	Use your ambition to motivate yourself
Give instructions to help a group task	✔		✔
Guide other people			✔
Question to secure a task objective	✔	✔	✔
Set an example	✔	✔	✔
Take a longer-term view of things	✔	✔	✔
Take the initiative			✔
Show courage and determination			✔
Inspire the trust of others			✔
Empathize with others			✔
Organize others			✔

Time needed: 30 minutes

How to

Say to the leaders: this exercise will help you think about what leadership is for and what kinds of things we can be ambitious for. Most students will be familiar with the idea of **still picture** or **freeze frame**. Ask students to get into groups of three or four. Say: 'I'm going to give you the name of a place. When I've done that, you've got two seconds to freeze [mime] a picture, that shows that place.' Then give an easy starter such as: the beach; the school; the bus stop. Count down from ten, clap and they freeze. Unfreeze all students but leave those in one group. Have the students stand in a circle around the one image. Then ask comfort zone questions, such as: 'Where is this? Who do you think the people are?' **Comfort zone plus** questions take leaders towards the higher order thinking skills such as: 'guess what they are thinking? What might they be feeling? And, what point are they making with this picture.' **Power plenary**. Ask: 'What leadership skills did you use when you worked the image together?' Usually students think, trust, cooperation, collaboration. You may need to point out the leadership thinking. Empathetic thinking is important to foreground. 'When you wonder what the characters in the image are feeling, you are using an essential leadership skill. A good leader must try to see a situation from the point of view of other people. Next, introduce the idea of **time capsule freeze frames**. 'In your group, get ready to freeze a problem or crisis. This will be a past image. Next we'll work through a future image.' Then give them a situation such as: bullying; being told off by a parent or teacher; or loneliness. Again count down from ten, clap and freeze. Unfreeze all but one of the groups. Then form a **thought circle**. The group rings one image. Have each member of the circle give a response to what's happening. You can also have each member of the thought circle ask a question that the rest of the group can answer. Or you can hot seat one member of the image and have him or her answer in role, questions about what the group is doing and why they are doing it.

Now introduce the idea of **leadership ambition**. Say: 'Leaders get ambitious for other people. Where there is a problem, leaders imagine a better world, a solution. This is called: being ambitious for others. It can be used on a small scale or in a community or globally. So, go back to your groups and on my count down, freeze a solution image. Use your leadership ambition skills, imagine the difference, and imagine the change.' What happens when you count down, or play timed music – again, TV theme tunes work well because they are no longer than five minutes – is that students think with pace and urgency what the difference could be, how a solution could occur, what it might look like if it were different. Unfreeze and thought circle. Now have the group talk about the changes from the first image. Crucially, say: 'What do you think has happened here? How has this come about? What might have been said or felt or thought.' It is helpful to go back to the groups again and have students act out the events that might have happened between the crisis and the solution. Ask: 'What leadership skills were used here? Who by? Who might have shown leadership and didn't?' Hot seat anyone. Ask them what made them use their leadership skills and why?

Challenge

Discuss the notion of ambition. What do you want to do; what do you want to be? This can be done in the secret box: on slips of paper students anonymously write down the answers to these questions. You can add other questions such as: Why do you want to be different? Why do you want your leadership skills to improve? What is the point of ambition?

This allows discussion and change thinking to occur. Not all students will have considered that ambition can be for the positive improvement of others, that it can be altruistic.

Andy – Student voice

We worked though a situation where someone new to the school had no friends and was being picked on because they were different. So in the ambition pictures, we changed that. We talked about how hard it can be to get someone to think what it's like to be someone else. We used hot seating to do this best, really challenging the most difficult character until they changed their ways and thought about the other person. We even did a scene where the new character challenged the bully. We gave them advice on how to do this safely and without using fists. The best thing they said was 'You won't make me feel anything. Ever. I control my feelings and you can never get to them.' We thought this was good leadership, to help someone think like this and to think that you can choose who affects you and who doesn't.

Discussion points

- What does it mean to be ambitious for yourself? Is it only about money? Is it only about career?
- Can you be ambitious for others?
- Can you be ambitious for people you have never met?
- How small scale can ambition be? Can you be ambitious for a lesson or homework?

Leadership tip

Running right through this course is the theme of collective responsibility: leadership for a purpose; leadership for personal and collective change. This activity helps students think this through, helps them think positively about ambitions so that they think of themselves as ambitious for others.

Activity 11: 2–3–5

Help students' leadership skills grow by reflecting on them in an active, direct way.

	Positive influence over others	Positive influence over yourself	
	Using your personal integrity	Organize yourself	Use your ambition to motivate yourself
Give instructions to help a group task	✔		
Guide other people			✔
Question to secure a task objective			✔
Set an example	✔		✔
Take a longer-term view of things			
Take the initiative		✔	
Show courage and determination	✔		
Inspire the trust of others	✔		
Empathize with others	✔		
Organize others			

Time needed: 30 minutes

How to

Show students the retention curve (as shown in the figure opposite). Explain that the longer you learn without review, the less you are likely to remember and act on what you have done. Make the link between learning and action. Learning can be about making some change after reflection, thought and skill practice. These sessions are about preparing the ground for improving everyday life. Say: 'So, action makes the learning more memorable and retained for longer. And even if it doesn't go right first time, that's what happens in learning. Be pleased that you are having a go. Most of your peer group will be surprised and challenge your initiatives. Accept this as a sign of growth. It's when people aren't surprised by what you do that you know nothing is changing, things are as they always were and that's not what this course is about.' This activity can take place whenever you like in the course. It's good every so often when you want to consolidate. And, like all plenary activities, it can happen at the beginning, middle or end of a session, as you think best.

Say: 'Think of three ways in which you have changed.' Or 'Think of three things you have learned

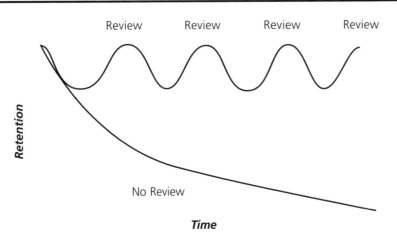

Review   Review   Review   Review

Retention

No Review

Time

The retention curve suggests that, without frequent review, knowledge learned has less chance of being retained over time

this week, or three things you want to learn, or three changes you have made.''You have **five** minutes to tell **two** people your **three** things.'You can say this to a background soundtrack. Many of them are five minutes or so long, TV sound tracks of action type programmes work well. Say: 'Stop when the song stops.' It gives a pace and drive to what the students are doing.

Challenge

It is crucial to include, at some stage, the demand that students reflect now what they want to achieve. So saying, 'Think of three skills you want to learn,' triggers this forward thinking and you can emphasize what a key leadership skill this is. Likewise, having students think of three skills they would like others to learn emphasizes the leadership skill of taking responsibility for others.

Tatyana – Student voice

Thinking of others was difficult at first. But the more we did this, the easier it got. We did this about every three sessions oo. It really helped us focus on what we had done and what we wanted to do. Leaders have to think about more people than themselves.

Discussion points

- What do you need to learn in the next **hour**?

This is such an important and difficult question. But it can open up a wide range of conversations about what the next hour requires, what skills we have, what we need and about priorities. Students will talk about the minutes getting to and from the lesson and what they need to do this well, and that's before they start to break down what they need in the lesson they are going to.

Leadership tip

This is a quick activity but be ready to let it take its own course into collective responsibility, how we learn, what skills have stuck and what haven't. It is key to stress, as the opportunity presents, that learners who are engaged in metacognition are likely to be more effective leaders. Do we shy from such pedagogic rhetoric? It will pay off. Students like the science of learning. They like being taken seriously and they'll use the terms we give in other contexts, with encouragement, at home or even in the canteen.

Learning to Lead © Graham Tyrer (Continuum 2010)

Activity 12: Affirmations – affirm your way to improved leadership skills

Affirmations are a tried and tested way to make small changes that add up to big differences in students' lives and in the lives of others. They can really work. It is a powerful process and has to be used carefully.

Positive influence over others	Positive influence over yourself		
	Using your personal integrity	Organize yourself	Use your ambition to motivate yourself
Give instructions to help a group task			
Guide other people		✔	✔
Question to secure a task objective			
Set an example			
Take a longer-term view of things			
Take the initiative		✔	✔
Show courage and determination		✔	✔
Inspire the trust of others		✔	✔
Empathize with others			
Organize others			

Time needed: 60 minutes

How to

Say to the group: 'You're going to be taught one of the most powerful leadership strategies. It can change your life. Many very successful leaders have been taught this and it has made a significant difference.' It helps if you've got a volunteer from the school or community who can testify to this, maybe even sharing affirmations he/she uses in everyday life.

There are the following rules to writing an affirmation:

- Imagine the future in the present tense, as if it has already happened.
- Keep your affirmation small, related to the next few days.
- Link it to a powerful emotion. Think of a time when you've experienced success, praise or encouragement.
- Reach to that feeling and use it to colour your affirmation.

Encourage spending time over this.

You will want to help the drafting process so the students don't set up false expectations. Story telling from your experiences helps if you feel comfortable doing so. Use a time when you felt yourself drawn to something you were thinking about – positively or negatively. We found it helpful to model the whole process, right up to showing the affirmation cards we had made.

Start with a practice. This involves asking the students to draft an affirmation in their homework planner. They can use bright fluorescent sticky notes and stress their temporary nature.

Then students think of a change they'd like to make for themselves in the next 24 to 36 hours, academically or personally. Examples include: wanting to feel more confident when walking into the tutor base; wanting the courage to put up their hand when they don't get an explanation in maths or English; bringing their equipment to class. Ask them to think of something just outside their experience but not too far. It's, again, the concept of comfort zone plus.

Next, ask them to imagine the improvement, as if it had already happened. Introduce them to the concept of seeing the future in the present tense. Model this for them in shared writing. Model the thinking aloud.

So, for example:

- I walk into the tutor base with confidence.
- I hold up my hand when I am stuck.
- I bring my pens and ruler and planner to school today.

Next, ask them to reach to an emotion they've felt when they were encouraged by someone or some event: scoring a goal; playing a part on stage to applause; succeeding in a test; and so on. Ask them to recall the emotion and reach into that emotion. It is called 'borrowing the feeling'. Say: 'Colour the affirmation with this feeling. Think of the words that describe what you felt. It shows you can be successful. It shows you have the potential.' Reassurance is important here. Some will say that they have never felt successful. Reassure them that there are times in everyone's life when success has happened. Say: 'Even being selected for this course is a sign of the belief others have in you. How did that feel when we said you had leadership potential? Use that feeling.' You may need to provide examples of vocabulary they might use. Tell the students that this is part of the literacy of leadership. So, words such as glad, elated, jubilant, pleased, thrilled, proud, happy, satisfied, all work well. We use an online thesaurus to generate possibilities. Next, students build the affirmation using their emotion word or words. So it becomes:

- I am delighted that I walk into the tutor base with confidence.
- I am pleased I hold up my hand when I am stuck.
- I am satisfied that I will bring my pens and ruler and planner to school today.

The key is to build realistic, achievable affirmations. Say: 'under-promise and overachieve'. Or, 'Surprise yourself with the everyday'. It is remarkable the effect it has on students when, eventually, after practice, they say that this does work, that this tends to help. And, although we emphasize the power of this strategy, we always stress that it helps. Say:. 'It doesn't cure, solve or transform on its own. It's one skill in the many we are building into our leadership skill set.' So, when they've written this simple, short-term affirmation on a sticky note, they attach it to the weekly page of their homework planner, or wherever they are likely to see it often over the next day or two.

Tell students again that repetition is key. Tell them to self-talk the affirmation when the mind is most receptive. This tends to be first and last thing in the day. Get the students together two days after this and ceremoniously 'allow the students to gift the affirmation to the group'. Word-process them into a display wherever you regularly meet, so the power of what they've done isn't lost, but they also don't have to worry about carrying the affirmation everywhere in this sticky note form.

Challenge

Students can then go on to push out further into comfort zone plus. The next affirmation can be about something more ingrained or a more challenging behaviour they would like to change. The timescale extends too. Push out to a week or five days. Step up the presentation of the affirmations. Have them write them on card or word process into their e-portfolio or homepage. Decoration is important. The colours they choose, the images they select to adorn the text are all important. They should feel something positive whenever they see the text.

Allow the students to choose an affirmation coach. This is someone from the group or a parent or tutor. This person encourages them to describe progress during the next five days. It helps to model this with a co-teacher or work with a volunteer student so they can hear you use questions, encouragement and thoughtful challenge to keep the affirmation's power alive.

Again, meeting after the agreed time period, as a group, can help unpack some of the successes and difficulties of repeating the text, thinking it and imagining it.

Aadarsh – Student voice

I wasn't sure at first. But then after a couple of goes, I could see that this self-talk has an influence. I use it all the time against myself, so why not use it for me? It was good that there wasn't forever to keep it going. The short time periods helped it happen. If we'd have been given a year to track it, it would have been difficult. But now, I do keep using this. And I've got quite long-term affirmations that I use for a few weeks at a time, about exams and dance.

Discussion points

- What is self-talk?
- When do you use it?
- Do you catch yourself talking yourself down?
- What are the first few steps away from talking yourself down?
- How can you help lead someone else carefully away from the habits of negative self-talk?

Leadership tip

This is about habits of leadership. What should be encouraged is incremental change. Give permission for backward steps; it can be quite pressurizing to think positively 100 per cent of the time. It's not possible. But for too many students they have never been shown that there are practical things they can do to re-engineer their thoughts more productively and positively. The affirmations are always a surprise to students. They are often sceptical at first but, with serious focus on the steps and review, supported in the whole group, they can be 'amazed by their potential'.

Activity 13: Take the money and run

A game to help students think about leadership motivation.

Positive influence over others	**Positive influence over yourself**		
	Using your personal integrity	Organize yourself	Use your ambition to motivate yourself
Give instructions to help a group task			
Guide other people	✔		
Question to secure a task objective	✔		
Set an example	✔		
Take a longer-term view of things			
Take the initiative	✔	✔	✔
Show courage and determination			✔
Inspire the trust of others			
Empathize with others	✔		✔
Organize others			

Time needed: 20 minutes

How to

A very simple game to lead into discussion about motivation for leadership, study and making personal progress learning. A copious supply of two-pence pieces is needed! Each person holds their palm flat behind their back. Place a two-pence piece in their palms. They then choose a space to stand in.

When you say 'The game begins', students have to walk around each other trying to capture as many coins as they can by lifting the coins from the upturned palms of the other students. Each person has held their palm up flat behind their back. The coins sit in the centre of their palms. The winner is the one who captures the most. It is a no-contact game. Players must not clench their hands to conceal the coin. If it's safe you can get the group to walk fast or run around.

As with all these games, it can, if you think it safe, be led by the students. The more you can encourage this the better. Give or discuss how this should be done. Even the minutia of where to stand so you can see everyone, who will adjudicate and how you celebrate the winner are important learning opportunities. Often these are more important than the game.

Challenge

Introduce the notion of the power plenary. Led by a student or group of students, who says: 'You have two minutes to think of three learning points and one question for the group about what people felt playing the game, taking the money, winning at the expense of others, your competitive sense, whether you wanted to win or not. In other words, how much does money motivate you? How far should we go to win at the expense of others' interests? I'm not going to make the connections between the game and leadership skills. This is up to you to find.' We find this is useful as a script on the screen or on laminated cards. Then, on the students' signal, the power plenary begins.

Put on a TV sound track lasting, say, two or three minutes. In that time, students have to exchange their thinking and ask their question of, say, two people. You can have a group feed back at the end but it's sometimes better to leave it there both for the sake of variety, but sometimes, if overused, the report back to class style of plenary can be a little false or disengaging for some students. We also call this thought exchange. Students seem to respond to activity such as this. It is good because the more learning activities become ritualized, the more they seem like heightened routines.

Michael – Student voice

We liked this. It's a quick fun game that gets you running around in the drama studio and makes you think. It's not easy leading a power plenary but you do feel important. We found it useful to get everyone standing in a circle and doing the thought exchange like that. I think the game teaches you to think about whether money is important or not. We thought it was funny that we would get so into a game that had two-pence pieces as the target. We also tried it with sticky notes and on each sticky we'd written an aim or ambition. Then the winner read them out and we talked about those we really admired or wish we'd said. People who wrote them said this made them feel important.

Discussion points

- What's important? Money or feelings when you keep coming to this course? Or a mixture of the two?
- Have students stand on a thought spectrum: money at one end, feeling at the other.
- They stand where on the line best represents their motivation; if someone stands where you wanted to stand, line up behind them.

Leadership tip

The game is a catalyst for thought, talk and action (TTA): one of the key processes of this course. Students create a space on their visual learning environment (VLE) e-portfolio for learning to lead where they could record their TTAs. It's like a learning log. The key was to use the Bloom list in the thinking verb grid (see page 138) and make the action short term, practical and not to worry if it didn't happen or happened differently. Leading to learn and leading to take action rather than being passive are the two key mantras of this work. So often the most simple, low-tech games open the door to deeper level thinking and edging towards change. It is so important that students see the possibility of taking great leaps but the probability of small steps.

Activity 14: Interviewing the guest

What makes a good leader? Find out from others what helps them lead.

Positive influence over others	**Positive influence over yourself**		
	Using your personal integrity	Organize yourself	Use your ambition to motivate yourself
Give instructions to help a group task	✔	✔	✔
Guide other people			
Question to secure a task objective	✔	✔	✔
Set an example	✔		✔
Take a longer-term view of things	✔	✔	
Take the initiative		✔	✔
Show courage and determination			
Inspire the trust of others			
Empathize with others	✔	✔	
Organize others	✔	✔	

Time needed: 25 minutes

How to

A parent, a cleaner, a TV executive, an actor, a footballer, a governor, a prefect, your best friend, all these people have different leadership stories to tell. Different students respond differently to each. Some felt distanced by celebrity actors, while some felt inspired. Some were surprised that the school admin assistants were asked for interviews, some were delighted because they knew them but didn't know them as leaders.

For this activity, students are reminded that a leader does two things. One, they positively influence others. Two, they positively influence themselves. These two routes lead to leaders in so many areas of life. All the possibilities were thought showered. Not all leaders are able to positively influence themselves and others all the time. And not all the time; we recognize that you can have off days, or even off hours. But sometimes, most times or occasionally, the evidence exists that dozens of people in the lives of our students have this skill. They don't necessarily know it and wouldn't call themselves leaders. But they are. It's so important that we help students redefine the concept of leadership. They too often think of figures in the public eye. And they are reassured when they see the skills are much closer to their grasp.

Of course, meeting people who have had great success in their lives is aspirational. The famous 'six degrees of separation' must surely be a reality. The governing body were asked who they knew and, before long, the trail took us to individuals in the media, sport, professionals such as airline pilots, builders and gardeners who had made a great deal of money, drove impressive cars and who could talk easily and in an informal manner with the students.

- School alumni are a good source. A gallery was made of people who had attended the school and were successful. There were photos of nurses, electricians, mothers, fathers, uncles, aunts, cousins, grandparents, footballers and so on, all of whom had led someone else, or themselves, to success of some sort.

It's fascinating to discuss the term success. Students need to learn that this is relative and that if you bring a smile to the face of a shy, diffident friend, you have had success. Even though tomorrow you feel like being invisible in the lives of others, first you probably aren't (there's no such thing) and second you have a right to be 'off duty' sometimes. These are young people. We can expect great things of them, but not the impossible.

The key is to get over the sense that we are responsible for our community. Without that idea being deep rooted, leadership is without moral purpose and possibly selfish.

The meetings were set up in a number of ways. Following are two:

Question Time: this works well when there are two or three visitors. A BBC iPlayer extract of the television series 'Question Time' is shown to the students, so they know what to do. The students prepare the questions, and they are vetted in a group. Then one of the students acts as the chair. A 'floor manager' helps pass the radio mike to the questioner and the 'show' begins. Limit this to an hour. It's very successful in a formal setting and with 'green room' refreshments afterwards. If participants agree, record it and use it in the term-end celebrations.

Thought Tracking: volunteer students sit alongside the 'guests'. When a question is asked, students go into role as the guest and give a reply. This can obviously be done in pairs in case one of them cries, because this is pretty challenging. But the effects can be significant. What's happening, of course, is that the students' leaders are putting themselves in the place of the leader guests and thinking through their responses. They are taking a small step in the right direction. The students choose a chair or chairs for the exercise and they moderate the activity and set ground rules around courtesy and politeness, both essential in leadership. Again, the displayed e-board discourse markers' scripts, that establish turn-taking phrases, are very useful. The most valuable we find are those that foreground listening; phrases such as 'could I just build on something Gary said?' or, ' I hear what Gary said and I disagree'. You can even point out the importance of the 'and' in this latter sentence, rather than 'but' to signal the importance of not negating someone's remark even though you may not agree. Key leadership skills are about organizing yourself, especially the leading with integrity strand and leading with empathy. All these small learning points are of key importance. We are taking small steps towards big goals. Again this has an acronym – **SSTBG** – and this could be displayed on the e-board too; the more these process ideas can seep into the dna of the course the better, so they know they have permission to make small steps rather than be overwhelmed with a false expectation to make sudden and, perhaps, unsustainable, giant leaps.

Challenge

Asking the students to invite guests can be so beneficial, since then they are learning about the kind of leaders they would like to learn from. This in itself helps redefine the often superficial notion of leadership, as students arrive with or feel reinforced by the media. Just be careful they don't over reach and get disappointed with a slow or negative response. This is the way of the world and often determination pays off. It is often found that many key national figures in politics and media are keen to get involved because of their interest in wider community cohesion. Universities also have a key role in widening participation, and students who haven't previously considered this route can find themselves made curious. Curiosity is an important aspect of learning. It seems easy. But it requires ingenuity, skill and allowing the planning to follow the direction of students' interest. For a teacher of leadership, piquing curiosity is one of the greatest achievements. Requiring students to follow a curriculum and requiring their compliance is important. But it's one of the steps that lead through the compliance, engagement, leadership spectrum referred to earlier.

Andy – Student voice

We met some really inspiring people who made us believe in ourselves and see that we could achieve so much. I think the people we got the most form were those who were closest to us. People who had been where we had, been to our school and taken the same exams and sat through the same lessons. They really knew what they were talking about and what it's like being us; meeting people's mums and dads from the course was good, especially when they came to our celebrations events at the start of the interview sessions. I really enjoyed the real thoughts. I could sense what it felt like to be these people; even people who had worked in areas really different to us, like in television or the web media or theatre. Working out what feelings they had or what decisions and questions they had had to answer made us think about our own situations and what we had to go through.

Discussion points

- What is success?
- What sacrifices have successful people had to make?
- What are the priorities of successful people?
- What can we learn about the attitude successful people have to others?

Leadership tip

This is such a good opportunity to introduce students to the idea that success comes in many forms. Having family members, alumni and colleagues from school tell their stories has a strong effect. Students often have a clichéd view of what success means. Having adults talk about **health, family and generosity** as things to which they aspire can come as a surprise.

Activity 15: The tick tock game

A game to help students lead others and think about personal and collective responsibility.

Positive influence over others	Positive influence over yourself		
	Using your personal integrity	Organize yourself	Use your ambition to motivate yourself
Give instructions to help a group task			
Guide other people	✔		
Question to secure a task objective		✔	
Set an example			✔
Take a longer-term view of things			
Take the initiative			
Show courage and determination			
Inspire the trust of others			
Empathize with others	✔		
Organize others	✔	✔	

Time needed: 15 minutes

How to

Start as if the game is a warm up. And if that's the mood of the group, use it as such. Take two pens. Pass one around the seated circle to your right. Say: 'This is a tick.' The person receiving it says, 'This is a what?' and passes it back to you.

You return it, saying, 'a tick'. The person passes it to her right, repeating the words, 'This is a tick.' The receiver passes it back, saying 'A what?' She passes it back to you saying, 'A what?' You return it, answering: 'A tick.' She passes it on saying, 'A tick.' The third person passes it on saying, 'This is a tick.' His receiver passes it back saying 'A what?' and so on back to you. And you start the movement back with the answer, 'A tick.' So the first pen is passed around the circle.

It sounds more complicated than it plays! It is a study in concentration, teamwork and group leadership. The rule, necessarily complicated, must not be broken. Pause the game and ask for a TRA: Thought, Reflection, Action. Say: 'What's this like? What in a lesson does this remind you of?' Often you get back reflections such as, 'When I have to learn something new and I don't see the point. I can't connect it to my life.' Ask: 'So what do you need?' and the leaders come back with: 'Patience, self belief' and, critically, 'trust.' And if they don't say any of these, draw them out.

Then start the same process to your left. Only this time, you say: 'This is a tock.' 'A what?' says your receiver. 'A tock,' you reply. He passes it to his left, saying, 'This is a tock.' 'A what?' says the receiver passing it back. 'A what?' says the first receiver passing it back to you. 'A tock,' you reply, passing it on.

So to your right, you have a tick being passed back and forth. To your left you have a tock starting its journey.

The whole group is involved in watching and listening – left and right, back and forth. They are leading each other. They have to be totally concentrated. One slip and the chain is broken.

Again, if it works for you, do a TRA: think what this is like in life, when you have to depend on someone. Reflect on when this happened to you? How could you have improved the situation? How could you act differently in the future?

The effect of the whole group working together keeping the tick tock going is helpful in getting students to think about the dynamics of group work. And when it goes awry, and it will, the no blame no shame ethos must apply. This is talked about a great deal in leadership learning: accountability yes; shame, no. The group wants to succeed and that's something to be encouraged.

Again, return to the collective responsibility value. You are responsible for the performance of the person next to you. This may sound a large leap from this simple game to the drama of this idea. But leadership learning is about taking the seemingly insignificant and making important parallels.

As ever, the key is thought, reflection action. What does it mean to be responsible for someone else? Can we think of someone to whom this applies? And what about total strangers?

Challenge

The tick tock metaphor can be related to a heartbeat and to clockwork. So, ask students' leaders to think of teams that work in this way: with passion and with efficiency. It is always amazing that students are capable of making the thought leaps this demands. Students talk about local and national charity groups, for instance. There is a hospice near the author's school and this led to the students making the link. One said: 'You have to work together to work for something bigger than you.' And a comment such as this makes the game worthwhile.

Ask the students to make a link: to think laterally.

Tatyana – Student voice

When we started, I thought, 'how will this work?' It seemed so complicated. But when we talked about it and found out how to make it work it was exciting to have the tick going one way and the tock going the other. It got fun when it crossed over. One person has to think both ways at once! But that's really interesting when you try to apply it to life and school and family. I thought about the people who look after me and what they have to go through, making sure everyone's happy in my family. They have to keep everyone happy and if someone isn't then we all have to lookout for them and not just depend on one person.

I remember playing the game and the 'cross over' person said, 'It's all down to me,' and yes it was. But someone else said, no, it's down to all of us. And that's true too. Perhaps more so.

Discussion points

- What does it mean to work together? What do you have to think about?
- Can you be responsible for someone else?
- What if someone lets you down? How can you help him or her?

This a difficult but important area of leadership. The advice the author gave was: you may be responsible for helping them but if they don't work with you, that's not your fault. If you can, ask someone who has made a mistake to think about what he or she did, think about what went wrong and ask, 'How can I repair this?' and you may be able to help him or her. A big ask? Yes. This is the challenge. And it is always reassuring and surprising how many young people are up to this challenge. They need a great deal of support and thought work to work this through, but that's what the group is there for!

Leadership tip

Of course, use the game in whatever way you want. Sometimes it takes 20 minutes, other times a whole session lasting an hour once students worked in small groups through some of the issues and done some TRA, pledging an action to make something work better for the greater good and thought through the issues of collective responsibility. Other times it is just fun! Laugh through the mistakes without taking it to any other level.

At yet other times the 'chemistry' of the group can be such that they want to perfect the process so that the chain doesn't break. Always enjoy it when this happens – like the power applaud. There can be a sense that 'We want to do this better than any other group in the history of learning to lead,' and encourage this friendly competition.

Activity 16: Leadership keys

A game to help students unlock their leadership potential.

	Positive influence over others	Positive influence over yourself	
	Using your personal integrity	Organize yourself	Use your ambition to motivate yourself
Give instructions to help a group task	✔	✔	
Guide other people			
Question to secure a task objective		✔	
Set an example	✔		✔
Take a longer-term view of things			
Take the initiative			✔
Show courage and determination		✔	
Inspire the trust of others			
Empathize with others			
Organize others	✔	✔	

Time needed: 20 minutes

How to

Place a set of keys on a chair in the centre of a circle of chairs. Leaders sit around the central chair. Say: 'The object is for the seeker to walk silently up to the keys, capture them and return to his place without the finder discovering this. The finder will be blindfolded and will point in your direction if she thinks she hears you. The finder has only three chances. The seeker wins if he gets back to his seat without being heard.'

Choose the seeker. Then, for following selections, pass the job to one of the students.

Play it for as long as you think its points are being made. Students usually enjoy the challenge, so stop it while they still want to play more.

Ask them to think about each level of the game. It may be helpful to take a plenary at each point of tension: when the seeker has being chosen; when he is half-way to the keys; when he is half-way back. Use these heightened moments to think. The game is about fun, but it's also about leadership progression.

Challenge

There are two challenges levels: first challenge level: when the keys have been found, say: 'We are going to pass the keys around the circle. When the keys reach you, you have two choices. One, you pass and say so, passing the keys to the person next to you. Two, for you to improve your leadership skills and potential, tell us what you want to unlock in yourself. Or tell us what you want to unlock in someone else, something that may be holding you back from developing your leadership ability.' The responses are a significant responsibility. A high level of trust and responsibility needs to be established. You must say that the group may not have answers because leaders don't always have answers, but leaders create confidence and a space to speak and reflect.

So, if a leader talks about, say, shyness as something he or she would like to unlock, you use the keys as a 'conch'. Say: 'If someone has a thought or response, you can have the keys and speak about the issue.' Remember that this is almost certainly a shared issue. And while you have the keys, no one else may speak.

Second challenge level: the seeker and the finder. These terms were chosen because they are so close. Ask the group: 'What do you want to find? What are you seeking?' The latter term is usually unfamiliar, so talk it through. Explain 'seeking' as looking for something you know is out there, but you don't know where it is. 'Finding' is more general. You may not know what you want to find, but you know you need something more in yourself.

Students who trust each other will talk about feeling insecurity in certain situations and would like to find an answer to this. Others will say that they have a definite change in mind, like being better at algebra or getting more organized.

When students have shared their insecurities, use the key as a 'conch' again. Say: 'If anyone knows they have a way forward for any of the issues they have just heard, raise your hand.' Then pass the keys to someone who has their hand raised and invite them to give a considered response. 'That's the virtue of the keys. For as long as you have them, you may not be interrupted, you can pause to think, you pass them on when you are ready.'

Natali – Student voice

The game itself is fun. And it's more difficult than it sounds. Even with one key, you think you can do it but it's not easy!

We liked the idea that if you had the keys no one could interrupt you. You could talk for as long as you wanted. It was new to us. And people were surprising when they shared thoughts about times, people and events that had 'turned a key' or shone a light on a problem or difficult time. People said things about people who had led them, people they had relied on, who opened doors, who believed in them. This last thing was so important. We decided that if you had the keys to someone's life, you had a huge responsibility to believe in them, to give them self-confidence because, in the end, no one can unlock things for you. You have to do it for yourself – with the help of others.

Learning to Lead © Graham Tyrer (Continuum 2010)

Discussion points

- What leadership skills did we need for this game to work? The focus areas here are working together so no one makes a sound that will confuse the finder and make it difficult for the seeker.
- Pause the game and ask the students to sense the levels of concentration. Ask why this is? It is usually high. Ask whether they experience this same level in an English lesson or maths lesson. Usually they will say no. Ask why, when what is being learned is so important.

Leadership tip

The game is a metaphor for significant events or areas of life and learning that students need to make progress. Some will say there is one thing they need, others are much more general. We found it useful to get into the area of whether there are 'keys to life', metaphoric 'doors' that have been closed or need to be opened. No matter what age, there is usually someone who will describe an event that had a significant effect on him or her, a moment when he or she understood something, when a teacher or parent explained something or reassured or gave him or her some advice that they have never forgotten. Other will say things are not like that for them. There are no significant moments, but slower, difficult to explain changes, either good or bad that have happened. It is important to stress the validity of either point of view.

Activity 17: Setting leadership targets

Understand that students need targets; this exercise will help them to work out what they need and how they can help themselves and others.

	Positive influence over others	Positive influence over yourself	
	Using your personal integrity	Organize yourself	Use your ambition to motivate yourself
Give instructions to help a group task	✔		
Guide other people		✔	✔
Question to secure a task objective		✔	✔
Set an example		✔	✔
Take a longer-term view of things			
Take the initiative		✔	
Show courage and determination			
Inspire the trust of others	✔		
Empathize with others		✔	
Organize others			

Time needed: 30 minutes

How to

Discuss first in a **power talk**, that is six minutes, to sound track music, the following: what makes a good personal target? How can you meet it? Who do you need to help you? This opens up the key issues.

   Then take each of the objectives as playing cards (see resource on the website: 'Leadership skill cards'). Say: 'Order the "deck" in any way you need. Make the top card your biggest need. Make the final card the area in which you feel most confident.' Then students take the top and lowest cards. Have them 'show their hands' (the two cards) to the group. Often opposites can be matched up; that is, those who have target needs matched by those who feel strong in the same areas. Next, agree a timescale. Shorter works best, say a week or a month. Then students choose a **target partner.** The job of the target partner is threefold:

- to encourage
- to give honest feedback
- to help find support.

Meeting a target involves leading yourself and leading someone else. We have a responsibility for each other.

Challenge

We teach **basic coaching rules** for the target partner and the leader. Our guidelines are these:

- ask
- challenge
- encourage.

Say: 'This is what an **ACE coach** does.' Tell the students that an ACE coach asks key questions, **C**hallenges the answers and **E**ncourages person development. Students ask the leaders what they want to achieve in the next two weeks in the area on their top card. Use questions to draw out of your leaders what they see and hear changing. The more strongly they visualize the change the more likely the leaders will be to make progress towards the target (stress 'making progress towards').

Say: 'Now challenge your **leader partners**. Invite them to see their change in as much detail as possible. Help them do this with questions about details in the room, in their book, in the relationship they may wish to change? What does it look like? What are you doing? Helping around the house becomes helping with something specific, on a particular day, with a particular person. Getting your homework in, becomes, think of a really important homework. Think of the day you have to hand it in. Which teacher, how do you do this? What do you hear when the teacher receives it? What do you see on your page when you have finished it? What do your parents say? How do you tick this off in the homework planner?

Say: 'Next you encourage the leaders. Suggest with them, things they could do, small steps into the **comfort zone plus**.' This is challenging, of course. To suggest small, imagined, visible, audible steps you could take is a skill acquired after practice. But that's what this course is about, to add to our skills, slowly and carefully. As ever, if the skill needs to be modelled with a volunteer or co-teacher, that's what is done.

Aadarsh – Student voice

We do a lot of target setting at school. So the playing card idea was good, unusual, especially the top and bottom cards. You didn't feel you were a failure. Everyone helped someone else. And because the time was limited you didn't have to keep it going for ever. It's good having a target partner because they look out for you for the two weeks or whatever you decide. They support you and, at the end, it's good to hear from other target partners what they did for their leaders. You are always surprised at the effort people have put into supporting and giving advice and things that can help.

Discussion points

- What kind of targets worked best?
- How did you go about getting support for your target? What helped you the most?
- How did you stay encouraged?

- What questions help when you are being supported by your target partner?

Leadership tip

It's the supportiveness of leadership that's important here. The short, achievable steps are key; students taking responsibility for leading one another is part of the excitement. Helping students to see leadership as cooperating, collaborating with someone else to achieve their goals surprises any students whose clichéd view of leadership is this: a leader gets everyone to do what he or she wants. We challenge this by having students see that a leader brings talents out of others, helps someone else plan, review and think through their next steps.

Activity 18: Leadership observation games

These simple and fun games will help students to think like a leader.

Positive influence over others	Positive influence over yourself		
	Using your personal integrity	Organize yourself	Use your ambition to motivate yourself
Give instructions to help a group task	✔	✔	
Guide other people			
Question to secure a task objective			
Set an example	✔		
Take a longer-term view of things			
Take the initiative			
Show courage and determination			
Inspire the trust of others			
Empathize with others	✔	✔	
Organize others		✔	

Time needed: about 10 minutes each

How to

Hands on your watch. Say to leaders: 'Without looking, try to think about the watch you are wearing. When I say 'now' tell the person next to you what it looks like.' Most students find this easy and, therefore, encouraging. They know whether or not they are wearing a watch and most are not! Those that are can describe whether it is digital or analogue, what its make is, what colour it is and so on. Congratulate them for having this basic observation skill. Say: 'this is what leaders are good at, noticing details. These can be details about what people are wearing and what that might tell you. But also details about how people are thinking and feeling.'

Fire extinguisher. A much more surprising and important observation game. Have students close their eyes. Then when you say 'Go', they point, eyes shut, to the place in the room where they think the fire extinguisher is. Then ask the students to open their eyes, still pointing to where they think it is. It always amazes them. Some will have pointed to the opposite place. Some won't have pointed, believing there to have been no such object. A few will have got it right. Often there is no extinguisher and this allows you to discuss important points about what we take for granted and what might save our lives if we take notice. Say: 'A leader has to assess the situation, notice what is priority. Don't worry if you missed it or got it wrong. In the next exercises, you may well improve this leadership skill.'

People watching. Say: 'Look really closely around the room, at others, at yourself, at the room. In a moment I'm going to ask you a question or two about what you observe.' Give leaders a couple of minutes. No more. Then say, 'Close your eyes. Now answer these questions. How many people in the room are wearing glasses? Raise your hand when I reach the number you guessed. Keep your eyes closed.' Then do this. Reach about three. Then have students open their eyes. They are always amazed. Treat with 'celebrity status' students with glasses! Make the point that even the most obvious and important details can be missed, and how important this is for understanding people. Reassure them that even though they may have missed this detail, they will improve through the final games.

Colours in the room. Again, invite students to look around the space. This time, ask them to notice colour. Colours of walls, displays, windows, clothes, shoes, books, whatever happens to be in your classroom. Then have students answer your observation questions, again with eyes closed, so keep your questions as few as possible. Say: 'Raise your hand when I reach the number you agree with. The colour green. Here are four examples of the colour green.' Do the same with other colours, each time having students open their eyes and check their answers. More and more will get it right. More and more will observe closely and feel more confident. There will be a few who don't. We ask each other to give advice. What helps observation? Why is it important?

Challenge

- Look out for anything red in 24 hours. You will see things you hadn't noticed before.
- Look out for anything unusual or different in the way people act, speak or listen. You will notice more details about behaviour than you had before.
- On your e-portfolio, or learning log, keep a record of anything you find new or surprising. You may notice as a leader, things you want to change or ask questions about.

Michael – Student voice

It is important a leader to look and think about where you are; too many things are take for granted. I was amazed by the fire extinguisher game; these things can save your life. I pointed in one direction, sure I'd seen one. But when I opened my eyes, not only was I pointing in the wrong direction but also there wasn't one at all. This made me think about what I take for granted in people, in situations I go through every day, what am I missing? I remember the next day thinking I'd paid more attention to my family, and noticed how tired my mum was and thinking what can I do about that, how could I help?

Learning to Lead © Graham Tyrer (Continuum 2010)

Discussion points

- What is leadership for? It's a huge question. But sometimes it needs to be asked. This simple game opens up the issue. What are we observing in people and why? The focus seems to be on understanding the way people think and feel. Understand the way someone sits, stands, looks, can help you decentre yourself and think about the way you speak, work with them or plan with them.
- What is important to observe in places?
- What is important to observe in people, in what they say, the way they dress, the way they stand, move? It is always surprising how 'naturally' instinctive most young people are to these paralinguistic signals. The key here is draw to their attention their acquired skills and those they need to develop. They think they know spaces and they need to see them afresh. More importantly, they think they know people, they can see them for more than they had assumed.

Leadership tip

Observation is about knowing and understanding others and their situations. Being sympathetic to what's happening around you is a key step to doing something creative and imaginative about what you observe. Leaders will see that they can't afford to miss anything. That details are important; some will reflect on details about themselves and others; some will see that if they have missed small things, such as the way someone dresses, they may have missed important factors such as how people think and feel.

Activity 19: Shaping up for leadership

A game to help students learn to take control.

	Positive influence over others	Positive influence over yourself	
	Using your personal integrity	Organize yourself	Use your ambition to motivate yourself
Give instructions to help a group task	✔		
Guide other people	✔	✔	✔
Question to secure a task objective	✔	✔	
Set an example			
Take a longer-term view of things			
Take the initiative		✔	
Show courage and determination			
Inspire the trust of others			
Empathize with others	✔	✔	✔
Organize others	✔	✔	✔

Time needed: 30 minutes

How to

Ask leaders to score their self-confidence from 1–5, 5 being high. We call this the **high five test**. Tell leaders they will score again at the end and they don't have to tell anyone. But they could use their e-portfolio learning log to record how they felt and what changed during the game.

This sets up the creative tension. Say: 'You are going to be in charge of groups of students. You will direct them, with speed and purpose and politeness: three key ingredients of leadership.' The game works as follows:

1. Students stand in a space of their own.

2. When the leader says a shape – square, triangle, circle or whatever you wish – the leader counts down from five to zero and the whole group has to organize into the shape the leader gives.

3. The leader explains the game and what will happen. Again, display the **discourse markers** you will need: 'I would like you to . . . get ready to . . . thank you for being courteous to each other . . . imagine the shape . . . use assertive language not bossy . . . lead don't push . . . guide, don't embarrass'.

4. Power plenary. It often helps just before the game is about to begin or just before it reaches a conclusion or other key moment, to stop, think and reflect. **Pause for a power plenary.** Ask leaders to suggest other phrases of leadership (or phrases of power).

Give reward phrases if the whole group has worked well together. Model for the leader how to single out students who have led well, without bossiness and pushiness, and with courtesy and assertiveness. Talk about what assertive means. Use a **physical spectrum** to illustrate the difference between some instruction phrases and others. That is: take two chairs. Set them ten feet apart. Stand at one end and ask: 'What would be an assertive phrase when you are getting others to form the shape?' Then move towards the other chair. Stop, say: 'Twice: once in the middle when the language has become off-puttingly bossy and then right at the far end when no one would follow you because you have become over bearing.' Again, have a student scribe, who will type up the power phrases that help students feel encouraged for display, even simple things such as: 'You did that really well/I couldn't have done it so thoughtfully/you were so helpful when you/thank you for thanking.' What we are trying to encourage is an ethos of encouraging, assertive support.

Choose a new leader and play again. This time have the group work in smaller groups of, say, five. Make it competitive. Invite the leader to encourage competitiveness and still keep it fun. Again, think through the phrases.

Now do another **high five test**. Invite students to discuss what has helped their self-score to improve. Have them identify other students who have helped promote their confidence and leadership – phrases such as: you can do it/we believe in you/you know you can.

Challenge

If the game is played in silence it can work really well. It requires strong assertive gestures, eye contact and shape. Agree signals, such as, the raising of hands to get silence or leader claps twice group claps twice means 'freeze'.

Andy – Student voice

You really had to think about organizing people quickly. Finding the right phrase to say at the right time was a challenge. Using the PowerPoint® display with key phrases on it helped.

Discussion points

- How can we get things done while still being polite and courteous?
- Why is it important to think of others' feelings when we are giving instructions?

Leadership tip

Sometimes use the word **power** to get students used to the concept that leaders have power to make positive change in themselves and others; power to bring about confidence in themselves and others; power to imagine a better next hour, day, week, future; or power to help, be generous, thoughtful, empathetic. There are misuses of power. These are worth talking about: the bully over-steps the mark. The leader is altruistic. The bully is selfish.

It's a good game for getting plenty of students engaged in leadership. The game leadership can change three times. In the small group version there are as many leaders as there are groups and, if you play it three times, ten or so students have experienced active leadership.

Talk about the **leadership of acceptance**. **Giving authority** to the person chosen to lead is key and, some say, is leadership itself.

Activity 20: Power rounds

A fun game to help students use leadership and challenge others.

Positive influence over others	**Positive influence over yourself**		
	Using your personal integrity	Organize yourself	Use your ambition to motivate yourself
Give instructions to help a group task	✔	✔	✔
Guide other people	✔	✔	✔
Question to secure a task objective			
Set an example			
Take a longer-term view of things			
Take the initiative			
Show courage and determination			
Inspire the trust of others			
Empathize with others			
Organize others	✔	✔	✔

Time needed: 10 minutes

How to

Say: 'there is a record for this activity. I wonder if you will beat it. It will require three or four leadership skills. I wonder if you can tell what they are?' Then explain the game. The leaders sit in a perfect circle. Then you pass a clap around, starting with you and passing it to your right. Everyone has one clap in turn and it finishes with you. Work as quickly as you can around the circle and everyone has to have a turn in order. Ask students to guess the fastest possible time. Then say: 'I've not known it done in faster than one and a half seconds. It can be done in this time.' And it can! The students are up for the challenge. Then, just before you begin, without a count, building tension, do a power plenary. Ask for a quick think. 'What skills are we going to need?' The **leadership language display** will help. Students say skills such as collaboration, cooperation, team work and listening. These are all key leadership skills. Draw attention, if these come up, to the difference between them and the clichés of leadership: telling others what to do and bossing people around.

Game begins. Usually allow students three attempts. Each of the others are led by students.

Then the single sound. Say: 'The better we are as leaders the more the sound of this next clap will be unbroken. Watch my hands. When I count down, I'll clap once and you do the same. No one gets left behind.'

Again, power plenary. Just before you start. Ask for a quick reflection (or 'QR' – it is often helpful to shortcut to these abbreviations as it shows they've internalized the learning strategies. Every small metacognitive act builds better leadership. And students feel as though they own a code, adding to the sense of a team). 'What will we need to be successful?' The count down and go. Try again if it was untidy. When you get one clear sound let another leader lead.

Say to the students, 'OK, we can do this without a count down.' QR and they'll say things such as 'We'll have to watch carefully,' and then draw out from then that they are passing authority to the leader, letting her lead; this helps her leadership and is an act of leadership on their part.

Challenge

This game works with counting rounds, or alphabet rounds, or colour rounds. They are good to start a session, encouraging concentration and reflection on the skills of collective leadership.

It also gives you opportunity to teach applause. This may sound obvious. But you can talk about when this should happen, what it means and how not to over use it. There are ways of giving applause as a gift without simply using it as a sound. When something worth it has happened, we say: 'Will applause leader now tell us no more than three things that we have done well or an individual who has done well. Then we'll gift an applause. QR.' Name the leader and he explains the reasons before the reward. Give positive feedback for courteous, appropriate conduct.

Tatyana – Student voice

We had no idea it could be done so quickly. But it can. We got it to one and a half seconds. We got the colour round to three seconds because it's harder but it doesn't matter if you repeat or even if you make up a colour. I said 'grupurple' and people knew what I meant! I like leading applause. It makes you feel important to tell the group they did well at something and have them congratulate each other. It's what leaders do.

Discussion points

- How did you get others to do what you wanted?
- What did it feel like to have them follow your lead?
- Discuss the idea of responsibility. How easy is it to respond to this? Interestingly, most students say they have no problems with leading the group through a round. So you can expand this into a discussion about times this day when you had to take responsibility for an activity. There will be many times from the mundane when they were asked to pass out the books in class through to some who may have led an activity in sports. They may not have explored the idea before.

As has been said, taking responsibility for yourself and at the highest level are key, making it a matter of routine that you take responsibility for others, perhaps even others you have never met.

Leadership tip

This simple game has a number of key leadership elements: it allows the group to build the skills of two or three leaders; and it allows you to point out that passing authority to someone else is an act of collaborative leadership. Drawing out the skills of someone else is what leaders do.

Activity 21: Mission impossible

Nothing is impossible. This game helps students to boost others' self-confidence.

Positive influence over others	Positive influence over yourself		
	Using your personal integrity	Organize yourself	Use your ambition to motivate yourself
Give instructions to help a group task		✔	
Guide other people			
Question to secure a task objective			
Set an example	✔	✔	
Take a longer-term view of things		✔	
Take the initiative			
Show courage and determination			
Inspire the trust of others	✔	✔	
Empathize with others			
Organize others	✔	✔	

Time needed: 30 minutes

How to

This game helps teach the importance of taking small steps to big goals. It helps leaders think about being realistic and about celebrating small successes.

Talk about the amazing skills a child develops so quickly: the development of talk, language, and reading, about how much develops over a small space of time. Use 'amazing facts' such as:

Your ribs move about 5 million times a year: every time you breathe!
One-quarter of the bones in your body, are in your feet!
The first known transfusion of blood was performed as early as 1667, when Jean-Baptiste, transfused two pints of blood from a sheep to a young man.

Fingernails grow nearly four times faster than toenails!

The present population of 6 billion plus people of the world is predicted to become 15 billion by 2080.

Women blink nearly twice as much as men.

Months that begin on a Sunday will always have a Friday the 13th.

Coca-Cola would be green if colouring weren't added to it.

On average, a hedgehog's heart beats 300 times a minute.

More people are killed each year by bee stings than from snake bites.

The average lead pencil will draw a line 35 miles long or write approximately 50,000 English words.

Camels have three eyelids, to protect their eyes from blowing sand.

The placement of a donkey's eyes in its head enables it to see all four feet at all times!

You're born with 300 bones, but by the time you become an adult, you only have 206.

Some worms will eat themselves if they can't find any food!

Dolphins sleep with one eye open!

It is impossible to sneeze with your eyes open.

The longest recorded flight of a chicken is 13 seconds.

Queen Elizabeth I regarded herself as a paragon of cleanliness. She declared that she bathed once every three months, whether she needed it or not.

Slugs have four noses.

Owls are the only birds that can see the colour blue.

A man named Charles Osborne had the hiccups for 69 years!

A giraffe can clean its ears with its 21-inch tongue!

The average person laughs ten times a day!

An ostrich's eye is bigger than its brain.

Ask students to sort the above into possible and impossible. Then reveal that they are *all not just possible but true*.

The point is, that what may seem impossible can come true.

Do a secret box, inviting students to anonymously put on a slip of paper one fact about themselves that they find amazing, or one achievement that has amazed them, no matter how small. Always say that these are going to be read out; and stress that it's not a guessing game. 'Your identity will not be revealed unless you want it to.' Often, students do want to share a story or some background. And always there's at least one story that amazes or surprises the group.

Next the students must set a mission. Start with something easy, just to make them smile. In pairs, A asks B to stand on one leg and count backwards from ten. B adds to this with one more mission, stand on one leg, count backwards from ten and tell me your favourite colour. The key is that students know that what they set their partner, they will have to do themselves. So you empathize. You ask them to do what is possible.

Eventually, one partnership will be left. Discuss why. Why are they the only ones left? The answer usually is that they thought carefully about leading each other, thinking through what could be achieved by their partner.

Challenge

Invite the partnership to set a mission for each other to be completed in 24 hours. The game requires partners to think through what could be achieved and what would be beneficial to the partner or to someone she knows. Say: 'Think small. For example, your mission is to tell a teacher when you don't understand something in a lesson where you are normally a little shy.'

Learning to Lead © Graham Tyrer (Continuum 2010)

Natali – Student voice

My mission was to speak to at least three people in my tutor group who aren't in my friendship group. I had to say one good thing about them. It was really hard and I had to ask around for things because I didn't know them. But it made me think: what if everyone did this sometimes? Getting a compliment because of a bit of research shows you were really being thought about. Leader put others in the centre of their attention.

Discussion points

- What did you have to think about when you were setting a mission?
- What stopped you from setting something impossible?
- What are the best types of missions to set?

Leadership tip

The game gets leaders thinking about **stretching each other's expectations**. Key to leadership is helping the people around them to want more for each other and themselves without getting discouraged. It is an act of responsible leadership to **think through the limits other people impose on themselves that can be removed or challenged**.

Activity 22: Virtual you

Students should lead themselves thoughtfully when dealing with other people. This activity gives them the chance to explore safe responses to people they may have difficulty with.

	Positive influence over yourself		
Positive influence over others	Using your personal integrity	Organize yourself	Use your ambition to motivate yourself
Give instructions to help a group task			
Guide other people			
Question to secure a task objective			
Set an example			
Take a longer-term view of things	✔	✔	✔
Take the initiative			
Show courage and determination			
Inspire the trust of others	✔	✔	✔
Empathize with others	✔	✔	✔
Organize others			

How to

Ask the group to think of how many times that day they have been positive to someone else, to their face. Often it will be very few times. Sometimes, hardly at all. Say to the group: 'Good leaders need to show others how important positive reinforcement can be.' Place an empty chair in the middle of the circle. Say: 'The chair is my virtual person. Who do you think I am talking to?' Say something like: 'Here's what I think of you. I value you and I couldn't do without you. You help me when I'm down and you give me good ideas when I need them.' Then ask: 'Who do you think I was talking to?' students will suggest relatives and friends. Then you say: 'I'd prefer to keep the identity to myself. But I don't often say those things to that person.' You can go further and say that you hardly ever or never share your feelings like this.' Tell the group that it's strangely easier to talk to the empty chair than to the real person.

Students pair up and take an empty chair. They imagine and don't reveal the identity of someone they want to say something positive to. If it makes them feel even more comfortable, they can sticky note the comment and place it on the chair instead. The partner can read it.

Aadarsh – Student voice

I spoke to my 'virtual' mum in ways I don't usually and that night when I got home, I tried a few words like the ones I'd used and my mum was so surprised. She said what had brought that on and I told her it was what we did in learning to lead. She asked me why I don't say things like that more often. I said I wished I did and I would try to do that.

Challenge

The partner becomes the person being spoken to. This works much better if it's the positive comment. The partner can go into role and give some feedback. Even if it's only to thank their partner, it's a powerful moment for both.

Again, having the leadership language display helps. Positive phrases do not always come naturally to all students. Encourage phrases that start with: 'what I've always wanted to say is/I wish I had the courage to tell you/thank you for/when you (give an example) it helps me to be better at/the support you give me.' Using imagery can help many students: 'You are like my foundation/my light/my star/my compass.'

Discussion

- Why do we keep our good thoughts about someone to ourselves?
- Do we need an excuse for telling someone how they support us?
- Why is this good leadership?

Leadership tip

Leaders need to change the atmosphere of a classroom, home, bus queue, wherever they are. After all, if you don't do it, who will? Leaders can model for others the kind of talk and behaviour to others that we need to see and hear more of.

The empty chair makes students less inhibited. Not revealing the identity also helps. Often students want to play to a real person and in that case their partner steps in. It's fascinating when this happens and the partner gives some sort of response.

Activity 23: Responsibility orbits

Learn how to feel responsible for each other.

	Positive influence over others	**Positive influence over yourself**	
	Using your personal integrity	Organize yourself	Use your ambition to motivate yourself
Give instructions to help a group task			
Guide other people	✔	✔	
Question to secure a task objective			
Set an example		✔	
Take a longer-term view of things	✔	✔	✔
Take the initiative			
Show courage and determination		✔	
Inspire the trust of others			
Empathize with others	✔	✔	✔
Organize others			

Time needed: 20 minutes

How to

Ask students: 'Who do you feel responsible for? What does it mean to be responsible?' Most students equate this with 'looking out for' or 'looking after'. It comes fairly easily for most students to do this for friends and even family. But for someone they don't really know? That's where this game pushes leaders into comfort zone plus.

Make a still, living picture with one person standing at the centre of the room and add people standing in further and further **responsibility orbits**. Ask: 'Best friend. What orbit should they be in? Parent? Neighbour?' Use 'should' to avoid students having to reveal aspects of their life. The point is that there's no right answer. Everyone is sharing views and perceptions. But, as always, encourage the view that everyone should be responsible for people they do not know. People in the neighbourhood, region and beyond. Do not encourage a sense of guilt, but do strengthen the connections between people, even though they have differences of geography, culture and time.

When a student is asked to represent someone from a different country in need of food and water, the students will place that person in a close orbit. And there is often a debate about whether the orbit should be closer or as close as friends and family. The physicality of the exercise helps them to discuss and think through the issues.

Challenge

Put the names of the group into the secret box. One by one, students select a name without looking at the name first. Model what to do if you get a name of someone you don't know well. It's important there should be a welcoming of whichever name you get. 'We are now in responsibility orbits with the person whose name we have chosen. This will last one week. Next, discuss with your partner one thing you would like help with that you think your partner can do for you. This can be help with a subject or a friendship issue. Commit to one, two or three things you will try to do to help. Write these down in the other person's planner. Sign it and date it.'

Michael – Student voice

I changed my mind about three times about where the orbits should go. At first I wanted my family closest of all. Then my best friend and then I thought about people who have very little and I thought whether they should be closest of all. And we also talked about people we didn't know in school. Where should their orbits be? You can't be responsible for everyone all the time. **What we decided was that once you knew someone needed your help, you shouldn't ignore the need.** Even if you can't help right away, you should try or get someone else.

Discussion points

- How far should you go to help someone?
- What is the job of the leader? To give answers? Or to help others think?
- What was the help you got from your partner?
- How did it change things for you?
- Did it help you solve problems in the future?
- Are you more able as a result of the leadership you were given?

Clearly, what we want to avoid is a sense of being reliant on the help of others. Leadership is about capability and building this in others.

Leadership tip

Once students have been introduced to the responsibility orbits idea, you can return to it and reinforce the ideas. Throughout leadership learning we return to the idea in various ways. It is so important that students give consideration to their growth in this area: even thinking about people you don't know is a prelude to action. Such an action is an important sign of leadership, in that you feel your skills and attitudes can improve the lives of someone you have not met.

How to Lead Others

Activity 24: Who's leading?

This game will help students to develop the voice and confidence of a leader.

Positive influence over others	Positive influence over yourself		
	Using your personal integrity	Organize yourself	Use your ambition to motivate yourself
Give instructions to help a group task	✔	✔	✔
Guide other people			
Question to secure a task objective			
Set an example	✔	✔	
Take a longer-term view of things			
Take the initiative		✔	✔
Show courage and determination		✔	✔
Inspire the trust of others			
Empathize with others	✔	✔	
Organize others	✔	✔	✔

Time needed: 30 minutes

How to

Say: 'This game will help you to think about what your voice needs to be like as a leader, how to use your body language as a leader and how to get the group on your side.' It is a very simple game. To help the learning, punctuate the activity with several plenary moments of reflection and action.

Incidentally, the idea of a plenary being reflection and action is key. Having students think through the games and activities in terms of these questions is important: what have we just done? What have we learned? What are we going to do with this?

So, the students sit in a circle. Have one of them volunteer to go outside. Call him the chooser. While he's gone, the rest of the group decides who's going to lead them. With this person chosen, you then explain the rules: 'Whatever the leader does, you copy her. The way she sits, the way she moves. Try to keep together. Try to move in exact synchrony.' The chooser is then allowed back in. Next explain to the chooser that he has to find the leader. Say: 'The game begins.' The leader makes her first move. It's better if it's small so the others can copy easily. The chooser has as many guesses as the game will sustain.

Plenary whenever you want, but good points are cliffhangers. The moment before you tell the chooser whether his guess is right. Then go through the three-step plenary: think, reflect, act. Better still, have another member of the group lead the plenary, asking the group to go into pairs and reflect-act.

Usually three guesses are enough. It doesn't matter whether the chooser gets it right or not. You can discuss a range of leadership points. If the leader disguised her moves well, you can talk about such issues as what it takes to keep people with you. Raise the idea that leaders don't leave anyone behind.

A central metaphor is that leaders are often careful not to be obvious. They let others seem as if they are leading, so much so that they end up working together seamlessly, without anyone knowing who is driving a process or project. It isn't easy to spot the leader in a well-led team. This is so important. If it doesn't arise in plenary, draw the point out. Students often have an impression that leadership is always overt and obvious.

Challenge

Have two leaders. This simple change makes it much more challenging. The leaders have to watch each other and lead together. Usually they take turns moving, without agreeing verbally.

This sort of tacit co-leadership is a stretch for most students to grasp but important when we challenge the superficial notion of the 'attention seeking' view of leadership. This game is about the opposite, the leader de-foregrounding themselves. It allows you to get into democratic, even dispersed leadership.

Tatyana – Student voice

Some of us thought leaders had to just tell people how to behave, how to act. But we talked about following by example. The game is about doing what I do, not what I say. We found that in schools leaders are not just the obvious people. Sometimes we want to follow quiet people who have a sort of character about them.

Discussion points

- When do we get our friends to do what we say and when do we ask them to follow our example? Is this always right?
- Are there times when people simply have to be told what to do? Does this bring problems?
- What does it take to put yourself in the background? What did it feel like to lead in this way, trying not to be obvious?
- If you were the chooser, what was your self-talk when you were watching the group? How did you try to spot the leader? What gave her away? What does that tell you?

Leadership tip

How often in life do we think that if leaders had acted with more empathy, by shifting perspective, they'd have been more successful? This game is about the leader decentring themselves, seeing themselves through the eyes of the chooser, not making any sudden moves or making moves no one can follow easily. It's a powerful symbol for the team building, collegiate leader.

Activity 25: Who's moved?

A simple leadership observation game. Leaders notice people around them and they think about how to help, understand and guide them.

	Positive influence over yourself		
Positive influence over others	Using your personal integrity	Organize yourself	Use your ambition to motivate yourself
Give instructions to help a group task			
Guide other people		✔	
Question to secure a task objective			
Set an example	✔	✔	
Take a longer-term view of things			
Take the initiative			
Show courage and determination			
Inspire the trust of others			
Empathize with others	✔	✔	✔
Organize others	✔	✔	✔

Time needed: 10 minutes

How to

Say: 'One person will leave the room after first making a mental picture of who's sitting where. Then, while they are out of the room, two people (or more) will have moved (or moved position). When the leader returns, he will have ten seconds from when he has sat down to say what changed while he was out of the room.'

Challenge

'Try challenging people's expectations of you. Think about a routine you have slipped into in your everyday life. A lesson where you always hand your homework in late, for example. Try to challenge those expectations. Make a conscious effort to choose something where you think you'll get a surprised reaction. Plan for this. Write it down in your planner and tell someone what you're going to do.'

Natali – Student voice

We all wanted to play this. We all thought we could lead it easily. But it's more difficult than you think. Only about half of us got it right. That made us think about what we're missing in everyday life. What changes are going on that we don't see?

Discussion points

- What did you find helped when you were observing?
- Were you surprised by anything you had to observe?

Leadership tip

This challenge is an opportunity for significant personal leadership. Give guidance that the timescale should be short, a day or two at most.

Activity 26: Leadership minefield

This is well worth the effort of rearranging the classroom. The effect of the sticky note activity is sharpened by having cleared the minefield and watched others carefully negotiate the obstacles. When students lead the whole activity, it builds careful discussion skills and positive listening.

Positive influence over others	Positive influence over yourself		
	Using your personal integrity	Organize yourself	Use your ambition to motivate yourself
Give instructions to help a group task			
Guide other people	✔	✔	
Question to secure a task objective			
Set an example	✔	✔	
Take a longer-term view of things			
Take the initiative			
Show courage and determination			
Inspire the trust of others	✔	✔	
Empathize with others	✔	✔	
Organize others	✔	✔	✔

Time needed: 20 minutes

How to

Explain that the activity is a kind of metaphor for leadership. Invite the students to think what this might mean. Invite them to think during the activity how it links with leadership.

First, ask students to write on separate sticky notes, up to three obstacles to leadership: students might discuss these first. They might come up with 'When people don't listen to each other', 'Lack of trust', and 'Not knowing what to say'.

Next, students stick these down in a random but even spacing over a defined area of the floor. Students pair off and half of them stand at one end of the classroom, the other half at the other end, standing opposite their partners. Leader partners test to see if they can be heard. You may need to explain assertive voice techniques such as carefully pronouncing consonants, vocalizing the last letters of each word, and the difference between projection and shouting. Explain that the object is to guide your partner through the minefield. If you touch a sticky note, you explode! On your signal, students use their voices to guide their partners who have their eyes closed, across the minefield. When they reach the other side, they congratulate their leader. Students then exchange roles and and are guided once more through the minefield.

Next, have each student stand near a group of sticky notes. In turn, invite a student to lift one from the floor and read it out. The group then discusses possible solutions. If these seem practical and realistic, the 'mine' has been 'defused' and the sticky note can be put into the bin.

Some notes take longer to defuse. Most require care, thought and delicacy. Some may have to be kept at the end of the activity on a notice board for later defusing. This is valuable because it suggests solutions are not always straightforward and do require careful consideration.

Challenge

Sticky notes can be used as questions to real-life leadership issues students have faced. 'What do I do if someone won't do what I ask?' 'What's the best thing to do if I see someone smoking in the bus queue?' Once again, these can be used as obstacles and then discussed after the exercise.

Aadarsh – Student voice

I found this really useful for problem solving and we've used it two or three times after that, like when we were preparing to become prefects. I felt better about the problems we were likely to face through being guided through them. Even when you were out, you could watch what techniques others were using to get their partners across. After, we talked about the best ones. These were often those who took their time, thought about it and paused to get more time to think.

When I led this game I felt a great sense of responsibility, especially when I was running the discussion afterwards. I had to be careful to get the group to decide whether solutions would work and not just tell people what I thought.

Discussion points

- What did you notice about the instructions you gave? How did the lack of time change your orders?
- Praise your partner for careful listening. How did you concentrate on your leader?
- Why is this a metaphor for leadership? What situations require you to guide someone through difficult times, events or problems?

Leadership tip

When discussing solutions to the sticky notes, tell students there may not be quick, easy answers. Sometimes the best solutions don't come straightaway but require time and reflection. This is part of being a good leader. Ask students to discuss interdependently; build and connect students' ideas together to illustrate the strength of collective problem solving.

Activity 27: Using leadership talk frames

This activity will help students to speak and write like a leader.

Positive influence over others	Positive influence over yourself		
	Using your personal integrity	Organize yourself	Use your ambition to motivate yourself
Give instructions to help a group task	✔	✔	✔
Guide other people			
Question to secure a task objective	✔	✔	✔
Set an example			
Take a longer-term view of things	✔	✔	✔
Take the initiative			
Show courage and determination			
Inspire the trust of others	✔	✔	✔
Empathize with others	✔	✔	✔
Organize others			

Time needed: 30 minutes

How to

Teach the language of persuasion. Have leaders give a two-minute speech to the rest of the group about any aspect of school, social or wider life that catches their interest. The author used YouTube models of speeches by Barack Obama and Martin Luther King, and then taught through modelling, each of the following ten rhetorical skills.

Say: 'Try to use any of the following skills.' For modelling, try to persuade the group that homework should be extended.

Emotive language and visualization

Ask the listeners to picture a future you would like or you would like to avoid. Try to play on their emotions. E.g.: 'Imagine this: you have no grades and no chance in life because you have not studied enough.'

Elaborate/heightened imagery

Ask the listeners to imagine something they will find aspirational. Use vivid descriptions so they use as many senses as you can evoke. E.g.: 'A family yet to be born is dependent on your grades. You work for them. Hear their thanks as they pay back to you in gratitude the time you have spent on homework. See the smiles on their faces. Hear the laughter in their voices.'

Facts and objectivity

Using research can help persuade a listener. It can be research you have done or work attributed to others. Either way, numbers, percentages and dates lend credibility to your point. E.g.: 'In a survey done in this school only two months ago, 90 per cent of young people aged between 11 and 18 said they thought school work would benefit their later success in life. A further 91 per cent said that learning independently would improve lifelong learning skills and thus increase life chances.'

Alliteration

Use this skill occasionally and with subtlety. It works towards the end of a paragraph or the end of the speech. Use a few phrases in which keywords begin with the same letters: the effect will be to make these words memorable. E.g.: 'We want our learning to be exciting, enjoyable and encouraging. Homework plays a part in making this happen.'

Rhetorical questioning

Have your audience agree with you. It helps when you are making controversial arguments. E.g.: 'Do we want young people to leave school with no grades? Do we want learning to last? Do we want our schools to be places of achievement?'

Repetition

This helps when you want your arguments to resonate and be retained. An aspect of this is 'the rule of three', in which you make three points in quick succession for vivid emphasis. E.g.: 'Our young people must be educated, they must be highly skilled and they must be free of fear. Homework helps deliver these outcomes.'

Structure: recency and primacy

Many students miss the importance of clearly signposting their arguments. E.g.: Give the listener a sense of the 'big picture'; make points that connect and save your most persuasive points for the beginning and end.

Refer to what we call '**primacy** and **recency**': i.e. what we remember most appears at the **beginning (primacy)** and the **end (recency)** of a talk or lesson or speech.

Logical connectives – cohesion

Use phrases and words that help you make your point and help you build your arguments. E.g.: 'You may want to live in a school where you get low grades. **However**, I'm sure you want better achievement and better life chances. **Therefore**, think about what homework really does for you. **On the other hand,** you could just ignore the issue, do no work and watch your grades fall.'We use a range of talk phrases that have this effect. See the **leadership connectives resource sheet** (on the website) that is used in the leadership language display at the start of sessions such as this.

Person and tense

Person: if you use 'we' you include your audience. 'I' makes you sound more personal. 'You' can help form a link between you and your audience.

Tense: switching between tenses can help your audience feel you know what things were like, you know what they are like now and you know what things could be like. E.g.: 'In the past, you did not like homework and found it dull. Now you see it has a purpose but you want improvements. If you work with me, homework can be something you enjoy, something you want to do, something through which you improve your grades.'

Repetition, antithesis and parallel phrasing

Repetition: by using this, you can lodge a keyword in the audience's memory. E.g.: 'Our homework should be helpful to do, helpful to our grades and helpful for our future.'

Antithesis: switch the sentence around half-way through. You can move an audience's thinking from where it is to where you want it to be. E.g.: 'Homework should not be meaningless, devoid of choice and apparently pointless; it could be full of enjoyment; a range of opportunities and help us remember what we need for the exam.'

Parallel phrasing: by using this technique, you create a memorable effect and have your audience remember a key point. E.g.: 'Do not say, "Homework will not improve my grades"; improve your grades by saying, "I will do better, smarter homework".'

Challenge

Invite the leaders to address a staff meeting or a student council with a proposal or a point of view. Have the students prepare, using any of the techniques modelled. The group offer supportive feedback, and two or three might like to attend the speech and give pointers for the future.

Michael – Student voice

I ended up talking to the leadership team about my proposals for better homework. I gave a five-minute speech about how it could be improved. Because it was short, I could get in many of the techniques so that made it sound really effective. I got an applause at the end and I felt I had been listened to and the techniques made it easier for the staff to remember what I said.

Discussion points

- What makes a good speaker?
- Who are the best speakers you know in your life and on TV? What do they do to persuade you?
- Consider how the best speakers stand, use their eye contact, hands and vocal variety.

Leadership tip

Essentially we are teaching a few skills of **rhetoric**. This is key knowledge for leaders. They can invent other techniques or research other techniques and choose audiences to address. Some students go on to develop podcasts or use the techniques when teaching others in group or personal challenges.

Activity 28: Three spheres of influence

Students are about to change others' lives. They can choose how they would like to influence others.

Positive influence over others	Positive influence over yourself		
	Using your personal integrity	Organize yourself	Use your ambition to motivate yourself
Give instructions to help a group task	✔		
Guide other people	✔	✔	✔
Question to secure a task objective			
Set an example			
Take a longer-term view of things	✔	✔	✔
Take the initiative			
Show courage and determination			
Inspire the trust of others			
Empathize with others	✔	✔	✔
Organize others			

Time needed: 45 minutes

How to

Ask: 'What type of a leader do you think you are becoming? Where do you think you, personally, can be effective?' Use the three spheres of influence. You can be influential in any one of three places. These are: **the spheres of present, past and future.**

Divide the group into three. Each group has the label of one of the three spheres of influence.

Set the following question: 'Think of three ways you can influence your sphere?' As a safe focus, you can choose the school.

The sphere of past

Students discuss:

- How has the school been seen in the past? Can this be changed with anything that happens now?
- Is there an event in the school's past that now seems different?
- Is there someone you found frightening in the past but now you think of differently?

Students come to see that the past is not fixed. It's a matter of how you see it.

The sphere of present

Students discuss:

- What is happening now that you can change?
- Who could you help today understand something or feel better?
- What could you improve in the way the school looks today?

Students will have less trouble seeing this as a sphere of influence. By now they will understand this as central to their emergent leadership skills.

The sphere of future

Students discuss:

- How would you like to see the school and how would you like others to see it? Remember, **you move towards what you think about.** Imagine as clearly as you can how you would like the image of the school to change in the next week, month and term.
- Think of someone you know who is trying to improve him/herself? How could you help them, even in a small way, to accomplish their goal, to bring about the future they want?
- Think of one subject you know you need to improve. What one small step could you take to make a change?
- One person from each group leads the sphere of influence. They are challenged to explain what they did, the questions they asked and some of the answers they came up with.
- Label each area with spheres of influence signage: past, present and future. Students are normally good at doing this. Before the session, task three students to produce the signs and laminate them on A3 paper.
- Finally, invite all students to take a tour. They visit each sphere zone in turn and hear from the sphere leader the summary of how they can be influential.
- Brief the sphere leaders to instruct their visitors using questions such as: 'Did you know how influential you can be? Did you know how you can influence the past/present/future? Let me tell you how.'

Challenge

Give each student three cards with past, present and future labels. Make the cards in circles to emphasize the point. Have them write one thing on each card relating to their own life. These can be put in the secret box and shared anonymously. This encourages students to feel they are not on their own in this journey to make change.

Andy – Student voice

What surprised most of us was how you can change all three spheres. Mostly you think you can't change much. Life sort of happens to you. But it made you think how you can even change the past – that's the hardest thing. It made me wonder whether I'd been right about what I'd thought about some people. I wondered if they thought differently about me.

Discussion points

- Leaders can change the past, present and future. How? Which is the easiest?
- Which sphere is the most important?
- How can leaders be in all three spheres at the same time?

Leadership tip

Influence is connected intimately with leadership. What so many students think is that they can only influence the next few minutes. Encouraging the view that leadership is about **taking responsibility for perception** is key. That is, you can decide how you respond to the present moment; you can redefine how you see the past so that you are released from its traps; and you can choose a future that motivates and drives you. One of the key insights this activity brings is that you are present in all three spheres at the same time. You can choose whether to be passive about this. Or you can choose to be a leader.

Activity 29: Each one teach one

E1T1 will help student's to improve someone's learning.

	Positive influence over yourself		
Positive influence over others	Using your personal integrity	Organize yourself	Use your ambition to motivate yourself
Give instructions to help a group task	✔		
Guide other people			
Question to secure a task objective	✔	✔	✔
Set an example			
Take a longer-term view of things	✔	✔	✔
Take the initiative			
Show courage and determination			
Inspire the trust of others	✔	✔	✔
Empathize with others			
Organize others	✔	✔	✔

Time needed: 20 minutes

How to

It is helpful to get students to remember these learning leader codes: E1T1 stands for 'each one teach one'.

First give a straightforward piece of content. This can be a list of **common spelling mistakes with the correct answers**.

For this exercise, the following words can be used: access, accommodation, achieve, across, aggressive, beginning, behaviour, calendar, changeable, character, chocolate, choice, committed, conscious, corridor, criticism, current, definitely.

Then discuss three ways of learning the correct spellings. Re-introduce the students to **VAK** (visual, auditory, kinesthetic). The group is divided into three: a visual, an auditory and a kinesthetic group.

Each group thinks of three ways of learning the words using that focus. Then sticky note the teaching ideas around the room.

Next group students as A and B. The As choose teaching ideas they like and deliver a five-minute lesson to their partner around the words.

Finally, feedback and **power plenary**. B shares how the learning went and compares the teaching ideas used with those available.

Challenge

Invite volunteer students to a staff briefing. Rehearse the students describing what E1T1 means. The students tell the staff that all the learning to lead (L2L) students have had basic training in this. If a teacher wants to use the E1T1 technique, the L2L students can explain it to the rest of the class.

It becomes even more of a challenge when the E1T1 becomes VAK E1T1. This encourages students to think more self-consciously about leading their metacognition. It also means they have a chance to discuss this with others. They should be encouraged to try different routes. Leaders of learning innovate and make mistakes but they take responsibility for supported learning about learning.

Tatyana – Student voice

Once we had talked with the staff, we found more and more teachers using the 'code'. It made for faster changes between activities. Where it's used, teachers don't have to spend ages explaining that they want everyone to teach someone something using VAK. They can just say, **'VAK E1T1'** and most people know what to do.

Discussion points

- Try this out in a lesson soon. See what learning style works best. Remember you can choose a style. No one style is best for any content or for any person. You make a decision based on what you are learning, what you are learning for and what you feel will work.
- Don't worry if one technique doesn't seem to have an effect. What does a leader do if this happens?
- Consider involving others in your lesson. With your teacher's permission, work in a group to plan a learning activity that will help it stick. You might find you invent a strategy that will surprise your teacher.
- Report back to the learning to lead group. What helped you make progress?
- What do you remember now from your lessons where you tried this?
- What has made it memorable? This is such an important question. The more you can identify what helps you learn, the better a learner you will become.

Leadership tip

Often students do not make the connection between learning and leading. This game helps them do the thinking. The staff meeting a challenge is important. It helps the leaders to feel they have offered a small and important change to the school's learning culture. We know, as teachers, that you never know something so well as when you have to teach it. So, getting E1T1 and VAK E1T1 as a routine in the school encourages more effective retention of content and skills. The learning to lead students sense an accomplishment if they have had a role to play in enabling better learning for all.

Activity 30: Safety valve

This game will help students learn assertive leadership when things have not gone the way they want.

Positive influence over others	**Positive influence over yourself**		
	Using your personal integrity	Organize yourself	Use your ambition to motivate yourself
Give instructions to help a group task	✔		
Guide other people			
Question to secure a task objective			
Set an example			
Take a longer-term view of things	✔	✔	✔
Take the initiative	✔	✔	✔
Show courage and determination	✔	✔	✔
Inspire the trust of others	✔	✔	✔
Empathize with others	✔	✔	✔
Organize others			

How to

Like 'Virtual you', this game uses the empty chair. Explain that this will make it easier to learn skills of **assertive challenge**.

There is a number of steps to assertive challenge that we use:

- Ask
- Respond
- Respond and explain
- Respond, explain and change.

We model this game first. Have the language display at the ready with a scribe on the keyboard adding new phrases as you go. Say: 'We are trying to add to, test and develop our repertoire of leadership language.' **Address the empty chair.** In your role play, choose someone real or invented who has disappointed you.

Say something like: 'First find out the facts. Ask questions. Be on safe ground before you respond.' Then respond. To the chair, say: 'Your actions are disappointing/surprising/confusing.' Explain: 'The rumour you spread has not helped.' Change: 'We need to put this right. This is not the real you.' There is a number of things going on here that attention should be drawn to in discussion.

It is the actions of the other person we are unhappy with. Not the person himself. A word such as 'surprising' implies things are not usually like this. Being explicit about the action needing change is part of assertiveness. Using 'we' implies there's help available. And the idea of a 'real you' suggests this action is uncharacteristic.

The mistake some leaders can make is to say 'this is just like you/you are always doing this/there you go again'. All this does is to reinforce the negative self-image the other person already has. It gives them permission to do the same again.

Katy – Student voice

I found it really helpful. I told the group this was a person in the last week who had lost my calculator when I lent it them. It may sound a small thing, but I trusted them and, at the time, I just didn't say much and bottled it up. So I felt worse. Being shown there were steps to change made me think how I'd do this differently.

Challenge

This game can take a number of important directions.

You can invite the leaders to express thoughts and emotions they may not have been able to say before. Say: 'As leaders we have a duty to think of three things:

1 Try to make positive change. Leaders change things for the better. Where a situation is broken, a leader tries to get it put right, not by doing it themselves, but by helping the other person to restore and, if possible, leave the situation better than when they found it. A leader goes 'the extra mile'. The leader tries to help the other person reflect on what they did. And, crucially, the leader tries to get the other person to put it right.

2 Look after yourself. You have a right to describe your emotions in calm, reflective tones.

3 Remember there may be reasons for the other person's behaviour, though not excuses.'

Invite the pair to role play the situation, that is, fill the empty chair. Give guidance that this needs considerable care. Make it clear by saying when the role play begins and when it must end. Many students find it helpful in a short role play like this to have a conversation. And, more often than not, these role plays end with an apology from the person in the chair.

Discussion

- What does assertive challenge mean?
- Should you tell someone else your emotions? When might this help? Again, we stress that the other person has no power over your emotions, but you may find it helpful to express what you felt.
- Should students have a part to play in sanctioning other students in school? Schools that operate restorative justice schemes do this.

Leadership tip

It is important to recognize that there will be times when people in a leader's life need to be challenged. The key is handling this carefully, thoughtfully and empathetically.

Activity 31: Conscience alley

An activity to help students to get others to think and talk about the needs of others.

	Positive influence over others	Positive influence over yourself	
	Using your personal integrity	Organize yourself	Use your ambition to motivate yourself
Give instructions to help a group task	✔	✔	✔
Guide other people	✔	✔	✔
Question to secure a task objective	✔	✔	✔
Set an example			
Take a longer-term view of things	✔	✔	
Take the initiative			
Show courage and determination			
Inspire the trust of others			✔
Empathize with others			
Organize others	✔		

Time needed: 20 minutes

How to

This game asks students to link leadership with thinking about moral and ethical issues; it allows them to talk about leadership in a day-to-day setting and, at a challenge level, thinking about local, even regional and global settings.

Invite students to do some research around the issue for the **alley**. It can be issue based. A good way in could be, 'Should homework be abolished?' Power think to, say, a five-minute deadline: in pairs, decide on two reasons for and two reasons against.

Again, use the **leadership language display** for thinking phrases such as: I think/I believe/it could be/perhaps/possibly/conceivably/definitely/imagine if/consider the situation that/in my judgement. All these help a leader become more reflective and assertive, and the more articulate the leader the more effective they will be.

Then divide the group in two. Say, 'A, you are going to give a reason why homework should be abolished. B, you're going to give a reason against.'

Then select a **chooser.** Say: 'You are going to lead our thinking.' The A line faces the B line in the alley and the chooser walks between each pair. Each person quietly gives their for or against reason. Why quietly? It adds a sense of intrigue. You find other students wanting to hear what's been said with an increased intensity.

Then when the chooser reaches the end she becomes the **convener.** It's an opportunity for another leadership role. The alley becomes a circle. The convener organizes this, asking for a perfect circle. She summarizes the points of view she has heard and gives a judgement. 'It's my considered view that . . .' Encourage a formal style; encourage tension at this point, delaying the final words taking a minute's power plenary. Ask for positive feedback for the leadership of the convener and the leadership skills required to think together.

Challenge

This can be particularly interesting when it's about a local issue, say whether there should be a road crossing near the school. Students are often resourceful about following up local websites and others such as www. Directgov.uk to find out what to do if you want such local change.

Thinking about local democracy is a challenge. Ask your local councillor to come and talk through the processes. This can lead to you getting an invite to the council chamber for a visit and a mock debate.

Andy – Student voice

Getting to go to the council chamber was so interesting. We had a 20-minute debate about whether there should be more police on the beat. And we had to think about whether people could change themselves, or whether we needed more discipline. We asked the councilor what these things cost and we found out where the money comes from. And we felt important and thought about what it means to be a leader in the area: it's difficult!

Discussion points

- What can we **help with**?
- What can we **influence**?
- What things can we **change**?

Leadership tip

Developing the leadership language display is so important. Often we assume students will have registers of leadership. Developing, together, slides around different generic aspects of leadership builds up their vocabulary over time. Thinking phrases, request phrases and instruction phrases – having them accessible through e-display to add to and use as scripts is an effective way of including students and enriching the quality of talk.

Talking about help, influence and change allows leaders to think about themselves, about events and about people around them. It is important they see the difference between all three and that they are capable of all three.

A point worth drawing out is that we influence and change everything simply by being present in the world. The leader makes a choice. The follower is simply passive.

Activity 32: Interview your partner as if they were a celebrity

This drama activity will show students how to have the confidence of an expert.

Positive influence over others	Positive influence over yourself		
	Using your personal integrity	Organize yourself	Use your ambition to motivate yourself
Give instructions to help a group task			
Guide other people			
Question to secure a task objective	✔	✔	✔
Set an example			
Take a longer-term view of things	✔	✔	✔
Take the initiative			
Show courage and determination			
Inspire the trust of others			
Empathize with others	✔	✔	✔
Organize others			

Time needed: 20 minutes

How to

Everyone puts their name on a slip of paper. Next to their name, they put a skill or an attitude about themselves of which they are proud. Many students are shy about this. But encourage them that no matter how small they think their accomplishment is, it is valued and appreciated. Say: 'What you think doesn't really matter, many others would envy it.' So even if students put something like, 'I have a good sense of humour', this is as important as the student who says 'I regularly get As in maths'.

Model the role play. Play a TV theme tune from a chat show. Have one of the students work with you as the guest. Have someone be the floor manager who 'warms up the studio audience'. Give them a script: 'You're going to meet her in a minute. You know you want to. You've come a long way to see her. Yes it's . . .' and encourage warm applause when the 'guest' joins you.

Model how to greet the guest. 'It's so great to see you. I've been looking forward to meeting you. I've heard so much about you. Let's give my guest a huge round of applause for what she's done.' Then introduce the skill or attitude on the slip of paper they have written. Give it a build up, no matter how modest it may appear. 'They have, wait for it, no, I can hardly believe it, they have achieved the skill of having a great sense of humour. How about that, ladies and gentlemen?' Remember this is all relative. Encouraging the students to realize that they are significant and so are their skills. They can finish the interview with this. It's the build up that matters. You don't need to get into detailed examples of their skills or draw stories from them.

You can set the exercise up so that the teacher is the floor manager. The guests stand by in front of their interviewers. The teacher plays intro music and then sound effect applause. There's plenty of sound effects available and it's very effective as the guest takes her seat and is welcomed effusively by the host interviewer.

The interviewer asks a few questions, then you count down, as floor manager, to the end of the show. Usually there's time to do this three times, so each guest has been welcomed with positive enthusiasm by three hosts.

Challenge

If the 'guest celebrity' can cope, take the questioning deeper so that others can see some of the reasons why the guest has become so successful. Punctuate this with supportive applause and reaction from the audience.

Natali – Student voice

You don't think you are a celebrity just for something like 'being friendly'. But the activity made me think about how some people find things very difficult that others find really easy. And it was great to hear yourself welcomed and greeted like a pop star three times in the activity. It sent you out of the workshop feeling someone special. That's important if I'm going to try and lead something or someone. I've got to believe in myself and value the talents I have because we've all got something.

Discussion points

- What does it feel like to be a celebrity?
- What skills do you take for granted in yourself?
- Try to list five reasons you are pleased to be you.

    This is a difficult one for many students. So break it down into five **life zones**: your learning, your feelings, your friends, your family and your future. Say: 'Think of one thing from each zone that makes you pleased.

Leadership tip

The learning to lead course is about drawing the best out of students and this is so often relative. We are helping students to value the relative differences they experience around them and we hope to model the kind of support we hope they will offer others. Most students are not far from this. They have all experienced 'put downs' from others and know this is better when reversed. There is something about the term 'leader' that gives students an excuse to draw out the strengths from others. Students say it's 'cool' to be seen as a leader.

Activity 33: The rule of the game

This game will help students to lead a group, ask the right questions and get others to do the same.

Positive influence over others	Positive influence over yourself		
	Using your personal integrity	Organize yourself	Use your ambition to motivate yourself
Give instructions to help a group task	✔	✔	✔
Guide other people			
Question to secure a task objective	✔	✔	✔
Set an example			
Take a longer-term view of things			
Take the initiative			
Show courage and determination			
Inspire the trust of others			
Empathize with others			
Organize others	✔	✔	✔

Time needed: 20 minutes

How to

A simple game you can take to whatever level you like. It can be used as a starter or the key activity of a session. Leaders sit in a circle. One leader is chosen as the chair. One leader volunteers to leave the room. The leaders in the room are tasked with thinking of about five questions they will ask anyone, at random when the leader outside returns, whose job is to discover what rule the group has agreed to. The rule must be obeyed before anyone speaks. It can be a physical rule, such as coughing slightly, or raising a hand or finger; or it can be a verbal rule. For instance the word 'because' must be used in the answer. The more bold the group, the more bold the rule. If the group thinks it can get away with it, using the word 'orange' or something equally unlikely will demand more verbal skill at building it in. The more extravagant the physical rule, the more likely it is to be spotted.

Learning to Lead © Graham Tyrer (Continuum 2010)

Try to let one of the group run the discussion that generates the rule. They must think ahead, visualize the game and decide what will work. The group must work well together, agree together and act together.

So, to draw this out, power plenary just before the game begins when the questioner has returned. Ask the group what leadership skills will be required. What will we have to show? And again, having the skills on e-display is key to helping them think this through and develop the register needed to internalize. The game is a means to this end.

Challenge

There's an opportunity to get into the difference between open and closed questions. The questioner will have a better chance of guessing the rule if the answer is longer: open questions require this. Stress that leaders are skilled at open questions.

Have students think of rules and about following rules. In threes, think of three rules it is essential people follow at school. If they can, think of the three rules that must always be obeyed.

Michael – Student voice

It's good fun guessing the rule and trying to increase the difficulty of getting away with more and more difficult rules to follow. We thought about how in life this is just the same. We follow rules when we don't see the point. And when we do this we are sort of leading. Doing something because you trust it's right, helps others, even when it doesn't benefit you straight away. Like walking on the left in the corridor is leadership because you're helping people you don't know to keep safe. They will never thank you. You do it because it's right. You lead the school even in small ways like that.

Discussion points

- What is the point of rules?
- How do you give authority to a leader, say a teacher in the class? Is it because of fear? Respect? Self interest?

Leadership tip

This game gets students thinking of the '**social contract**' of leadership. It's not just having rules that counts. It's the ability of the leader to get people to follow them. You can ask, 'How is it that we all followed rules in this game that didn't have any immediate benefit?' Students are often fascinated by realizing that authority is given to leaders, not simply taken; that the sheer weight of numbers in a class means that power is **given to, not taken, by the leader**.

The group is bound to get into rules that don't seem to make any sense and this allows you to share ways in which leaders communicate.

Activity 34: Leadership bridge

This will help students to give instructions to a group and help them gain people's confidence.

Positive influence over others	Positive influence over yourself		
	Using your personal integrity	Organize yourself	Use your ambition to motivate yourself
Give instructions to help a group task			
Guide other people			
Question to secure a task objective			
Set an example	✔	✔	✔
Take a longer-term view of things			
Take the initiative			
Show courage and determination			
Inspire the trust of others	✔	✔	✔
Empathize with others	✔	✔	✔
Organize others			

Time needed: 30 minutes

How to

Ask students to stand in two lines directly facing each other. They reach out their arms so that their fingertips are a couple of centimetres apart. Then demonstrate how to play. Say: 'I trust you so much that as I walk down between your lines, your arms will raise up in the air as I reach each pair.' You walk down and as you get to each pair, their arms go up until you reach the end. Then you congratulate them. Model the leader talk: 'Thank you. I felt safe. I felt that I could lead you. I felt part of a supportive team. And I felt led by you.' Then model walking at a quicker pace between the lines. Tell them this requires even more leadership from the group for you to feel safe and trusting.

Have one of the students lead the activity. He or she must ensure that the group have their arms up ready and when they judge it to be safe, they invite you to begin the walk.

The students will all want to walk or run themselves. This can be done quite quickly and requires very efficient group management. It's a test of the group's leadership.

If you think it's safe, allow one of the group to lead this part of the game. The students can peel off from one end, go to the head of the line, wait for the leader to judge it safe and give the invitation to go. Make sure that there's plenty of space at either end and no obstacles at the receiving end. In fact, that's where you stand to ensure maximum safety.

It can work like clockwork and we call it the **leadership bridge machine**.

Challenge

Say: 'As you walk down the line, each pair will give you a leadership skill.' They use one word or phrase from the leadership skill display or one they've learned. This can be a skill they think the leader actually has or one they 'gift' to the leader. When the leader gets to the end of the line, he can tell the group what skills he thinks he has; and what he thinks he has been gifted. This works especially well when used sparingly, that is choose someone who you feel, for whatever reason, needs the additional attention this gives.

Tatyana – Student voice

It was fascinating to hear which leader skills people gave me as gifts and which they thought I already had. You feel really good when you finish the line and everyone has been thinking about you because that doesn't happen in everyday life. And it's good getting skills as gifts. I tried to use some of them, like I got gifted the ability to make people listen to the teacher in a lesson. So I talked to the group about how I should do this. And they said things like make it to do with getting a good job. Someone said I should put a big picture of a Mercedes CLK on the board and take it down if people talked over the teacher. But I thought it would be better if I put it up when everyone was listening to each other. Anyway, I tried it. And the class said it was interesting to have the picture on the board when the teacher was teaching because it reminded them of what some people wanted in life.

Discussion points

- Use the metaphor of the **leadership bridge** and talk about what students need to achieve to improve their leadership from where they are to where they want to be.
- What do you most need to get these extra skills and abilities? Usually, one of the group will make the connection between the game and this question and say something like: 'What we most need is other people.'
- This game reinforces the idea that we improve each other, that we **open doors for each other**. Draw a parallel between the arms going up and the help others can give you. Discuss what this is like in everyday life.

  It can help to role play an event that links the game to the every day. Role plays about getting stuck trying to help someone listen to the teacher. Another leader in the class supplies the language that makes the difference.

Leadership tip

One of the key ideas of this game is to show how you can lead and be led at the same time.

It is helpful to tell the A line to **gift skills** and the B line to say what skills the line walker already had. That way it doesn't matter if there are repeats and it ensures the leader gets equal measures of reinforcement and encouragement.

Using the phrase '**I gift you**' allows students to safely encourage without pointing out something they feel might be lacking.

Learning to Lead © Graham Tyrer (Continuum 2010)

Activity 35: Three symbols listening activity

An activity to help students improve their leadership listening.

Positive influence over others	Positive influence over yourself		
	Using your personal integrity	Organize yourself	Use your ambition to motivate yourself
Give instructions to help a group task	✔		
Guide other people			
Question to secure a task objective	✔	✔	✔
Set an example	✔	✔	✔
Take a longer-term view of things	✔	✔	✔
Take the initiative			
Show courage and determination			
Inspire the trust of others			
Empathize with others	✔	✔	✔
Organize others			

Time needed: 30 minutes

How to

At the beginning, have the **Chinese character for listening** (available on the accompanying website) **posted around the room.** Don't say why. Invite guesses and curiosity. The key is that the character is a composite of three parts. **Listening is made up of listening with your heart; with your mind; with the whole of yourself.** Make the point that **leadership listening** is just that.

In pairs, have the students stand at opposite ends of the room in lines. Line A thinks of an instruction for playing a video game or a sports rule or something similar. This can be the soccer offside rule, for example. Challenge the students to think of something reasonably complicated.

Then, when you or your student co-leader begin the game, all the A leaders begin their instruction at the same time. After one minute, the B partners share what they heard. It gives a good opportunity to share some speaking skills such as using the last letters of every word, speaking from your diaphragm, speaking slowly and empathizing with the situation.

The listeners share what skills they needed. These include **filtering, focusing and feeding back**. A good listener must filter out noise and talk that isn't relevant to the task; focus on the speaker so that they feel important; and feedback constructively and clearly.

Next activity, have the students work in trios. Two leaders role play a problem: a best friend has broken your trust, or gone behind your back, spreading false rumours about you. A and B are the friends and try to resolve the issue. C is the rapporteur and at the end of the activity feeds back the quality of the listening.

At any time, share the significance of the Chinese character. But the key skills need discussing. Did the listening take account of feelings? Did the listening happen with thought? Did either of the characters listen without the whole of the self. One way we found to get this over was to model listening with your back to someone. Then slowly turn 180 degrees, asking the group to say at which point you are listening with the whole self. Often, good listeners make the other person feel that they are the only people who matter; and, crucially, leaders give time for the other person to talk without turning the talk back to themselves with phrases such as 'That's the same as happened to me' or 'I can top that'.

Challenge

Explain the **confirmation** listening skill. Whatever the other person says, deepen her understanding of the event she is describing or responding by using some of her own language and phrasing. They say, 'I felt betrayed when you spread that rumour.' The listener says: 'Tell me about the feeling of betrayal.' Don't deny the other person's experience but don't automatically assume it to be helpful to her predicament.

Through to **exploration.** Allow the other person to talk through the event in his own words. Reflect back his words, allowing him to hear himself, adjusting his perception if he wants. Listen, so that he steps outside himself. Ask him to see himself in the third person. This develops the other person's skills of self reflection so that he acknowledges his feelings but isn't ruled by them.

Into **resolution.** Accept this isn't always possible. Listen so that the other person guides himself to **options for action**: 'I could do this/we might say that/it's possible these things could happen'. Stress the good listener doesn't provide solutions but builds the skill of the other person to consider possibilities and think through the consequences. This is called the **CERtain process**: confirmation, exploration, resolution.

Sometimes it's helpful to talk about the theory that whatever someone feels is usually rational although not always acceptable. So, feeling angry about betrayal may well have a reason but the feeling can lead to corrosive responses. Where we want to get to is **the leader realizing she has choices over how she reacts and that leading oneself means making these choices; key to leading others means helping them to see this**.

Aadarsh – Student voice

It's really interesting to hear about how you can help people. The CERtain method really works. There's a way in which you can get someone to think about themselves. And it's interesting the Chinese character sums it up. Once it's been learned, notice how often when people talk they don't really listen with the whole of themselves. Often people listen and then use what they've been told as an excuse to talk about themselves. Funnily, teachers are better at this than many people. A lot of the group said how the best teachers made you feel important when they listened. Teachers are leaders.

Discussion points

- Ask others what they mean by listening.
- Is there a difference between hearing and listening? As a challenge, ask: 'Which of these has more to do with trying to understand?'

Leadership tip

Too often listening is selfish. It is an act begun to affirm the listener. However, truly well led, altruistic listening is a high-order skill. As a means for helping someone else develop the confidence, capacity and skills to make change, it is a key leadership attribute.

Activity 36: 5 + 10 = L

An activity to develop students' skills in leading change quickly and efficiently.

	Positive influence over others	**Positive influence over yourself**	
	Using your personal integrity	Organize yourself	Use your ambition to motivate yourself
Give instructions to help a group task		✔	
Guide other people		✔	
Question to secure a task objective		✔	
Set an example			
Take a longer-term view of things			
Take the initiative			
Show courage and determination	✔	✔	
Inspire the trust of others	✔	✔	
Empathize with others	✔	✔	✔
Organize others	✔	✔	✔

Time needed: 20 minutes

How to

Leaders stand in a space of their own. They close their eyes. Play some music, TV theme tunes work well because they are short, recognizable and usually add tempo. Say: 'Think of five ways this school could be improved. When the music stops, you'll have three minutes to tell ten people what you were thinking of. What you will find is that, each time you tell them, you'll get better at saying it quickly and you'll use language that is more to the point. Be assertive, polite and make sure you get your point across to ten people. Listen out for and try to remember as many ideas as you can that you get in return.' There's a real energy to the sharing when you begin this. Again, play music if it helps. We found calming music to work well, counterpointing the physical energy of telling ten people your thoughts.

So, the title of the game: five ideas, shared with ten people, equals leadership.

Crucially, you need to get someone to chair the discussion that follows. It can be a good idea to co-chair, so you can scaffold the chairing skills.

Ask: 'What are the best ideas? How shall they be communicated? Who will do this? When and how will we report back?'

Challenge

Invite someone from the school senior leadership to be present. This gives an incentive to the activity. Telling the group that there's a strong likelihood of change occurring motivates and secures engagement. At the very least, getting leadership feedback from such a guest will improve the skills of the group.

Natali – Student voice

We found this got a significant number of ideas round the group quickly. At first we wondered how we could do this in such a short time. But it's amazing how much can be done. It made us wonder how much time is actually wasted in longer discussions; the trick was to keep what you had to say to headlines and one bullet point. We learned this trick and it made the bullet point quite sharp.

Again, what we learned was how helpful it can be to use vision talk: a sentence with what the change will look like got results. Phrases like: imagine this or hear this or can you see this, made the listener remember and have a clear idea of what you were talking about.

Discussion points

- Can you see the future in the present?
- How much change is possible quickly?

What might change in a lesson and make a big difference? One student, for example, came up with the idea of homework always being set at the beginning of the lesson. He said, 'Imagine you were made curious by the homework. Imagine the lesson got you thinking rather than working.' We thought this was an efficient way of explaining.

We also call this activity **twitter leadership**: students understand how powerful brief acts of communication can be. There's no point trying to limit talk to a number of words or characters, but timing and limiting the number has the same effect.

Leadership tip

What is being modelled here are fast ways to energize the thinking process. Often school students don't believe they have the ability to think of change. Often they are surprised by the collective resource the group represents $5 + 10 = L$ reveals this capacity.

Of course, you can vary the numbers depending on the stage of your group. A less experienced group or with less time, can be $5 + 5 = L$ or whatever works for your circumstance. We found five ideas each worked and in a group of 25 produced 125 ideas of which about a dozen each time are useable that day. It's power leadership. 'There's not a moment to lose,' we say, ' and your explanation skills need to be decisive, incisive and relevant.' Incidentally, there's also the opposite timing. This is where you insist only one idea can come from a ten-minute talk. This requires students to be reflective and selective in their thinking. The 'code' for this is **$1 \times 10 = L$**. And in this activity it helps if the sharing is also slower, explaining in ten minutes to one other person. You use the same envisioning technique since we see

Learning to Lead © Graham Tyrer (Continuum 2010)

this as key to leadership: describe the vision, explain the benefits, and discuss the process. Again, having someone there who can set the wheels in motion helps emergent leaders see they can have some influence if their ideas are relevant and clear.

Activity 37: The organizer

This game will help students to organize and motivate someone they know.

Positive influence over others	**Positive influence over yourself**		
	Using your personal integrity	Organize yourself	Use your ambition to motivate yourself
Give instructions to help a group task	✔	✔	✔
Guide other people			
Question to secure a task objective		✔	✔
Set an example			
Take a longer-term view of things			
Take the initiative			
Show courage and determination			
Inspire the trust of others	✔	✔	✔
Empathize with others	✔	✔	✔
Organize others	✔	✔	✔

Time needed: 20 minutes

How to

Say: 'Organization is about motivation, self belief and support. You are all part of a team and some people realize this and some don't; sometimes the team works for you, sometimes you need to organize them.' Using play money, pin a £500 note at one end of the room. Then ask the students to stand in two groups. 'The leader must organize her group so that the £500 note passes from one person to another, without them moving, as quickly as possible from the far side of the room to you. Organize your team as you like.' The quickest way is a straight line, the straighter the better. Don't tell students this. Let them find it out. It's a powerful moment when they do. Give a signal and the person nearest the money reaches, takes it and passes it to the next person and so on to the leader.

Challenge

Two volunteers tell the group an ambition they have for the week. It is safer to suggest they offer a short-term goal.

They pin this up on the far side of the room the same as the money. They each have a team. Play the same game, only it's the ambition that is passed down.

Then ask: 'In life, who would these people in your group be that could help bring the ambition to you?' It's quite an eye-opener for the leaders as they connect the game to life in this simple way. Obvious solutions are reached: parents, friends. But less deep levels are reached when you say: 'Each member of the team must have a role to play.' So if there are ten people on the leaders' teams and the group has only thought of five individuals in the leaders' lives, press for more. There are dozens, of course, and make this point. Even though you have thought of ten, there may be a hundred or more who connect in some way to your leaders.

You can role play this too. The ambition is pinned back on the furthest wall. The group thinks of the order each role would play in delivering the ambition to the leader. It's a fascinating moment as you encourage the group to think, 'Who's closest to the ambition? Who should be top of the line? Who's closest to the leader?' The debate that follows is where the learning happens. Often, one group will suggest the parent is closest to the leader and in the other group it is a best friend, or even someone they don't currently trust who is blocking the ambition.

The role play goes like this: suppose the best friend is closest to the ambition slip. He says, 'I'm going to help by . . .' and the others in the line use this starter phrase or something similar, 'I'm on your side because . . .' 'I'll be on your team because . . .' and the ambition is passed down the line. This isn't a race any more. Stress this. The contributions must be thoughtful. We found this works well with team A watching team B and vice versa. It offers the chance for reflection and comment. 'What did you think was helpful in what was said? Who was the best leader in this person's life?'

Michael – Student voice

It was great to be part of the team that brought something the leader wanted to them. He chose as an ambition for the week, 'Standing up for himself'. I was a teacher in the line. So when I passed the slip, I said to the next person, 'Let him speak for himself, don't disrespect what he says.' And the person next to me in the line was a middy supervisor. And he said, in character, 'I'm going to look out for him and make sure other people aren't making him feel worthless.' Then the leader got us together and organized us. She told us what she wanted us to do, how she wanted us to help him. It was quite moving to hear him tell his teachers, in role, how they should explain things better and make him feel confident in class. The teachers asked, 'How should I do this?' and the leader said, 'When you ask us to put our hands up if we don't get it, really mean it. Sometimes we feel you are just saying it.' Then we talked about how we could make these points in real life. Then it got really interesting. We discussed having the confidence to tell a teacher how they could help. And later some people actually did this. When we met for another session we talked about the successes we had. Some had been brave enough and polite enough to do it. And there had been some good talks after class about getting more help.

Discussion points

- Who are the easiest people to organize?
- Who are the most important people to organize?
- Who could you help the most?
- How could you get on someone's team and lead him or her?

Leadership tip

The leader organizes thoughtfully, carefully and with empathy. You can't boss people around. But you can suggest to those in your lives that they help us. There's nothing selfish about expressing what you feel you need. The leadership skill is in doing this so that others are motivated to get involved. So the principle of win-win is important. What's in my interest is also in yours.

And here's the leadership key: **if you want something to improve in your life, you have to help someone else**. This is a real revelation for many students, that achieving something for yourself can benefit others.

Activity 38: Leader says

A simple game to help students develop a leadership voice and body language.

	Positive influence over others	Positive influence over yourself	
	Using your personal integrity	Organize yourself	Use your ambition to motivate yourself
Give instructions to help a group task		✔	
Guide other people			
Question to secure a task objective			
Set an example			
Take a longer-term view of things	✔	✔	✔
Take the initiative			
Show courage and determination	✔	✔	✔
Inspire the trust of others			
Empathize with others			
Organize others	✔	✔	✔

Time needed: 20 minutes

How to

Open with a **power talk** about how a leader should stand, sit, talk, look and use eye contact. Discuss what is called, **power eye contact**. Define it as holding someone's look for a fraction of a second longer than is socially necessary. Practice it briefly with a few volunteers, getting feedback from the leader and the led. Play with other forms of eye contact, either too long or too short: discus the effects. Students enjoy learning the fine nuances of this and it's a difficult issue for many, so volunteers are necessary.

Then, very simply, discuss and display discourse markers leaders should use when inviting others to follow him or her. Discuss the effects of phrases such as: I'd like you to, I invite you to, I want you to, I need you to, I insist you and so on. Important to talk here about the nuances. The merits of please and thank you are explored. Keep the talk focused and thoughtful. It's important to balance action and reflection.

Next, settle on three phrases/words that everyone agrees are generally important. Why? Usually leaders say things such as: they don't want to feel bossed around but they do want to feel led. They want the group to feel safe. They want the leader to feel trusted. So which phrases will help this? It differs from time to time. And so it should. These phrases become **power phrases**.

Then the game begins. The leader gives an instruction. But no one in the group should follow the instruction unless one of the power phrases has been given within this instruction. This encourages listening skills among the rest of the group and helps leaders think about the rhetoric and registers of leadership. They say: 'Please put one hand in the air. *I would like you to* raise one foot. *Thank you for* folding your arms.' If an instruction has been given without a power phrase it should be ignored. This will catch leaders out. They are 'out' of the game but not out of the process. They become rapporteurs. They give feedback on the quality of leadership, on the quality of instruction and listening from the rest of the group.

Challenge

Increase the speed of instruction so that it is harder to listen out for the power phrases and more important that these leadership discourse markers are paid attention to; ensure that the leadership of the game is passed to several leaders and not just the teacher. The more the operation of games like this can be facilitated by the teacher and not overtly led, the more the ethos of the course is promoted.

Michael – Student voice

It sounds like a simple game. But the more we talked about the language and body language signals needed to play it well and run it well, the more we developed our skills. We had to really think as a leader would. A leader pays attention to the detail of how someone speaks, how they react to the way a leader leads. The game allows you to think deeply about what it means to lead others. Plus it's quite good fun when everyone does what you say!

Discussion points

- Notice the way leaders you admire in daily contact and on TV make others feel safe and yet show how to work and learn. How do they do it? Notice the smallest things: the way they stand, the tone of voice they employ, the phrases they use a lot that others respond to.
- How did it feel to think about the small details of what to say?
- Which praise and instructions worked the best? That is, which ones caught out fewest people? It's thee instructions that are the best leadership cues. When people are surprised by what you say and do, you haven't made them feel secure and included.

Leadership tip

The game is all about paying attention to the smallest details of action and speech. It is what we ignore that matters most. What we take for granted, we should examine most closely, for it is these phrases, actions and behaviour that have soaked most deeply into the 'dna' of our thinking and values. This game helps nudge our thinking in this direction.

Activity 39: Triangle of direction

This game starts students thinking about three different sides to themselves and gets them to choose a direction.

	Positive influence over yourself		
Positive influence over others	Using your personal integrity	Organize yourself	Use your ambition to motivate yourself
Give instructions to help a group task	✔		
Guide other people			
Question to secure a task objective	✔	✔	✔
Set an example			
Take a longer-term view of things			
Take the initiative			
Show courage and determination			
Inspire the trust of others			
Empathize with others	✔	✔	✔
Organize others			

How to

The group divides into four. Each person thinks of a real life dilemma and sets it as a question like this: 'What would you do?' Give some examples:

- A teacher accuses you of something and you know you haven't done it.
- A student says you've stolen something of his and you know you haven't.
- Your best friend tells you that someone is picking on her in the year above.

Students write these dilemmas down and put them in the dilemma box. You need a box per group of four. Then the students choose one of the four to be the dilemma leader. They stand in the middle of the other three who form a triangle. One of the triangles offers the box and, at random, the dilemma leader chooses a slip of paper and reads it to the other three.

Next all the dilemma leaders in the room get together. They form a dilemma circle and choose a leader. The triangles stay as they are. The dilemma circle leader asks the group to share any three dilemmas and they plan a response. At the same time, the triangles think of the best solution they can.

After about ten minutes the groups of four reform. **The leader in the centre of the triangle becomes the person in the centre of the dilemma.** One of the triangles says: 'What will you do?' The dilemma leader gives her response.

The triangle can go into role as the others in the dilemma. This gives the opportunity for the dilemma leader to question, test and challenge them: 'Why did you go behind my back? What will it take for us to still be friends? How will you help me gain trust?' As a development, each part of the triangle is the same character, but three different sides. So, the dilemma leader says to one person: 'What does it feel like to have betrayed me?' then she turns to another person and asks another related question: 'What will you do to repair the trust?' Then give the instruction to open the triangles. The groups get back into to a circle. One student leads the plenary. It's important that there may not have been resolutions to all the dilemmas. Help the group to see that a leader attempts to bring people together, to see the different sides of a problem. A leader takes responsibility rather than ignoring a problem.

Andy – Student voice

It's so interesting being in the middle of the triangle. You do feel faced with different directions, characters and emotions. You feel responsible because you are in the middle of the problem. Having the dilemma circle helps because you've got people to take your issue to for a group think. I liked hot seating the different characters in the dilemma. The dilemma box made everyone wonder what would be in it and it made people think about real life situations.

Challenge

The triangle thinks of **three different solutions**, with one preferred. Then, when the dilemma leader returns from the dilemma circle, she is faced with three different directions. She questions and role plays as before. Finally, the dilemma leader chooses one of the three directions, or blends it with the idea she had.

This version emphasizes the complexity of dilemmas and, again, uses the power of the shape to emphasize this. The opening of the triangle at the end, suggests a moving on, but we stress that sometimes there is no easy way forward.

Discussion

- When should a leader intervene and when stay away?
- Should a leader ever ignore a problem someone else has?
- Do you have responsibility to more than just your friends and family?

Leadership tip

The point is that leaders collectively solve dilemmas, using role play, empathy and assertiveness. The shape of the triangle is unexpectedly resonant. And having the dilemma leader turn from one point to another reinforces the multifaceted nature of dilemmas.

Try to discuss when it's better to get someone else to help rather than trying to solve everything yourself. Sometimes exploration is better than solution.

Occasionally each dilemma leader goes to three other triangles and takes the dilemma for discussion. Then they return to their home group. Use this to make the point that the network has power. Of course, we also stress the issues of sensitivity and confidentiality.

Activity 40: Teacher in role

Some exercises to help students develop leadership questioning and response skills.

	Positive influence over others	Positive influence over yourself	
	Using your personal integrity	Organize yourself	Use your ambition to motivate yourself
Give instructions to help a group task	✔		
Guide other people	✔	✔	✔
Question to secure a task objective	✔	✔	✔
Set an example			
Take a longer-term view of things			
Take the initiative			
Show courage and determination	✔	✔	✔
Inspire the trust of others	✔	✔	✔
Empathize with others	✔	✔	✔
Organize others			

Time needed: 20–30 minutes

How to

We find this one of the most important skills in developing heightened focus in leadership development. Teacher in role doesn't mean putting on a voice or costume. It means showing an attitude. And less is more. The more students question, discuss, dialogue, the more we are developing their ability to lead someone from one attitude to another.

So, taking a low status role works well. E.g.: the new person in the tutor group. Start by saying: 'This drama will last about five or ten minutes. I will say when it has started and when it has begun. I won't tell you much about the situation. I want you to infer this. That's part of the skill, putting together clues and working out how to help, how to lead.' Brief one of the students to introduce you. He takes on the role of the form tutor. He says something like: 'This morning we welcome David to our group. I'll let him speak for himself. You will find he is a little shy at first. He had a difficult time at his last school.' Then you come into the circle. It's important to walk from outside the circle. It slightly intensifies the drama; try to get stillness as it begins: you can do this with your presence. Less is more. Play low status. Sit with the circle and allow questions to begin.

It can be a good idea to get the questions prepared beforehand. Explain the difference between open and closed questions and that, sometimes, closed questions are a good way to begin when people are nervous. It allows them to feel secure by getting the right answers, even the simplest can have reassuring effects. Have them ask things such as: 'What's you first name? Where do you come from? What hobbies do you have? Which team do you support? Do you have a favourite colour?' You can support this by giving brief, monosyllabic answers. This allows the group to feel they are being successful. Plenary, if you like. Signal you are coming out of role. 'I'm just going to pause the drama (or press pause).' Deepen the questions. Tell them you don't want advance warning so have them discuss, quietly so you can't overhear. The brief is to try and lead the new person into the group by giving confidence and accepting the person and showing them respect. As a whole group, you can give guidance about this, such as: 'Accept what they say but don't necessarily tolerate it.' There's a whole discussion topic here: the difference between acknowledging what someone says and challenging if necessary. Say: 'Challenge unacceptable attitudes assertively and politely if this happens.' The group will probably come up with courtesies such as welcoming and introducing the 'tutor group'. This is good leadership. You might need to teach, by modelled writing on a projector; script for doing this so they can all see them if they get stuck. Sometimes, students won't know how to greet, welcome and put at ease. Of course, this is a false situation in the sense that a student wouldn't be quizzed in this way in front of the whole class and this needs to be stated. We are grandstanding and practicing the kind of leadership talk likely to lead someone to confidence and strength.

Teacher in role means following the story created by the learning needs of the group. So, if you sense they need more help deepening the questioning, 'press pause' so you can discuss the kind of question that will help develop thinking and empathy. Phrases such as 'What can you remember . . .?' 'What are your favourite . . .?' through to highly challenging questions such as, 'what could we do to help you?' 'What if we . . .?'

Challenge

The teacher in role can then become a paired role play. It can help to fast forward to three days later. In pairs, interview each other. Ask what had helped or hindered the newcomer's integration into the school. In this way, again, we are asking students to imagine the future as if it had already happened. And solving problems that might have arisen. In the plenary, hindrances can be shared and acted through as forum theatre, that is, when for instance we act out the newcomer not being talked to at break, the group can collectively solve the problem by directly intervening. Putting your hand up stops the drama and you invite yourself in to contribute a question an invitation or some other intervention. And you can ask the group for advice before this happens. Finally you can hot-seat one of the newcomers and ask him/her for feedback on how well he or she was led by the group or their partner. Critiquing the leadership helps develop alternative strategies.

This also works in trios. One student acts as observer to the paired drama and gives feedback on how well the new comer was led.

Michael – Student voice

We all enjoyed the in role. Most of us like acting but those who don't played the observer. We found that our vocabulary was stretched and we didn't know some of the words in the leadership grid. But it didn't matter. Part of the exercise was to try out new words and see if they worked. This kind of situation happens a lot at school and many of us found afterwards that we took more interest in helping someone get used to and make the most of the new school.

Discussion points

- Do we have a responsibility for each other?
- Whether should that end?
- How do you step up to the challenge of helping an outsider fit in?
- What do we say to people who don't take an interest?
- How can we tell others it's cool to help people feel safe and wanted?

Leadership tip

As with so much leadership learning, the Bloom thinking skills taxonomy was found helpful in structuring the questions and thinking the leaders need to develop through drama. Sharing this explicitly, using the grid below, helped to improve the vocabulary of action and questions, especially when, in role, the 'tutor group' discussed what they could do in and around school to help the new student and new students generally. The Bloom taxonomy was used and innovation added as a high order leadership skill. The verbs next to each thinking skill can be used in many of the leadership activities. Return to them recursively so they gain in familiarity. It means here, for instance, that students can frame a leadership action using, say verbs of synthesis: 'We could create a space for people to go where they could feel safe.' Or, 'We could combine tutor tie with circle time to give newcomers a chance to speakeasy.' The teaching skill is in inviting students to experiment with a vocabulary that may not instantly fit. Comfort zone plus.

The simple grid on the website is useful. Different activities can be focused on around different elements. Again, using rule of three, only pick a maximum of three at a time when you use them and make one the challenge level.

This can easily then become a basis for actual action. Using the rule of three helps: 'What three things could we do this week?'

Knowledge	list, define, tell, describe, identify, show, label, collect, examine, tabulate, quote, name, who, when, where
Comprehension	summarize, describe, interpret, contrast, predict, associate, distinguish, estimate, differentiate, discuss, extend
Application	apply, demonstrate, calculate, complete, illustrate, show, solve, examine, modify, relate, change, classify, experiment, discover
Analysis	analyse, separate, order, explain, connect, classify, arrange, divide, compare, select, explain, infer
Synthesis	combine, integrate, modify, rearrange, substitute, plan, create, design, invent, what is it?, compose, formulate, prepare, generalize, rewrite
Evaluation	assess, decide, rank, grade, test, measure, recommend, convince, select, judge, explain, discriminate, support, conclude, compare
Innovation	what if, supposing, say, let's say, imagine, picture, envisage, visualize, see in your mind's eye, think of, consider, conceive of, create in your mind

Activity 41: Making change for real: the gift exchange

This will help students to think about leading change for real. What does real change in someone mean? Is it possible to make change last?

Positive influence over others	Positive influence over yourself		
	Using your personal integrity	Organize yourself	Use your ambition to motivate yourself
Give instructions to help a group task			
Guide other people			
Question to secure a task objective	✔	✔	✔
Set an example	✔	✔	✔
Take a longer-term view of things	✔	✔	✔
Take the initiative			
Show courage and determination			
Inspire the trust of others			
Empathize with others			
Organize others			

Time needed: 30 minutes

How to

Say, 'Leaders, I'd like you to think of one change in your daily life you'd like to make. Think of something small. Something you could actually do. Like getting your homework in on time tomorrow, or not ignoring that person in your tutor room, or being more pleasant to a particular teacher.' Give some refection time. Perhaps some paired time.

Then say: 'Now think of some change you'd like to give to someone else. Don't think of someone in particular in the group. Think of change that would help more than one person. Such as, being more organized; getting your school equipment ready the night before; not rushing your work in class. When you've thought of it, that's your leadership gift. In a moment you're going to give this to five people.' Have the students walk around the room meeting each other. Call this the leadership gift exchange with a greeting such as, 'I give you a leader gift: I give you the power to get your homework in on time.' Receive the gift from whoever you meet with thanks and move on. It's important to use the words, 'I give you the power' and it's important to thank your partner without disagreement or without rejection. Accept the gift, however improbable it seems. You never know when you might need it.

Challenge

Have students manage the change they have just gifted. In a leadership tutorial, three days later, get the students together and discuss what they gifted and what change has happened. Have them discuss in groups, in a power talk, what they could do to help each other, how they can look for the changes each wants to make, how they could assist and lead the changes they want to make.

Natali – Student voice

I was surprised that, by coincidence, I got the gift I was thinking of. I wanted to make sure I remembered my shoes not my trainers. I think people knew that and twice someone said it. But it shows people think about you and they don't miss much. When you say, 'This is a gift,' you have to say it seriously. It's hard to keep a straight face. But when everyone does, it really works. Because, in a short time, you get five gifts. And this is what leaders do. They build people up. And they keep it real!

Discussion points

- Did anyone get the gift they were thinking they needed?
- What gifts did you get?
- When do you think you will need what you were given?

Leadership tip

This is about leading carefully, thoughtfully and basing your leadership on practical change in the lives of other people. It's also about getting over the embarrassment of gifting change to someone else. It's key to students' leadership growth that they see it as important to empathize with others and have the courage to tell someone what they want for them. Tell students they do have a responsibility for each other. That's what this game is about.

Activity 42: Organize me

Students will learn how to organize themselves and others in a supportive and assertive way.

Positive influence over others		**Positive influence over yourself**	
	Using your personal integrity	Organize yourself	Use your ambition to motivate yourself
Give instructions to help a group task		✔	✔
Guide other people			
Question to secure a task objective			
Set an example		✔	✔
Take a longer-term view of things			
Take the initiative		✔	✔
Show courage and determination			
Inspire the trust of others			
Empathize with others			
Organize others			

Time needed: 20 minutes

How to

A leader empathizes. Discuss what this means. Think of three people in the room. Guess what they might be feeling about themselves. Tell your partner what you think, but don't name the person you were thinking about. Now do a round. Say the words or phrases you were thinking. Do any of them apply to you?

Now ask your partner if you can help him organize something simple and everyday, for example his homework diary or English book. Discuss what a leader might do in this situation. Leaders will empathize with their partner. The book or planner is his property: you will need to be sensitive about how you discuss it with him.

Praise what you can. Praise as much as you can. Leaders give deserved praise.

Use the leader question technique. Ask your partner what she thinks of anything that seems disorganized or incomplete. Ask your partner what she might do to improve it. Take it a stage further. If your partner is happy, get her to organize her school bag with you. Praise what you can. Edit with her what she doesn't need and what she does.

Additional idea

Have your partner meet you in two days and show her your planner or your schoolbag. Has she kept it organized? Again, praise what you can.

Katy – Student voice

It was difficult to show someone the mess of my bag. But I found it useful because my partner explained things clearly and thoughtfully. And when the teacher did a role play with someone to show how to do this, I found it useful to see how you can change someone through questions and praise.

Discussion points

- How can you give praise so that your partner really thinks you mean it? Think of your voice and eye contact. Say what you really mean, look your partner in the eye.

Leadership tip

Doing a role play first really helps. You need to show how to say what you mean and how to help people feel proud of what they can do right.

How to Lead Your Community

Activity 43: Conscience witness

Lead the thinking of others. This activity will help students grow in thinking of their friends and developing their sense of conscience.

Positive influence over others	Positive influence over yourself		
	Using your personal integrity	Organize yourself	Use your ambition to motivate yourself
Give instructions to help a group task	✔	✔	✔
Guide other people	✔	✔	✔
Question to secure a task objective			
Set an example			
Take a longer-term view of things			
Take the initiative	✔	✔	✔
Show courage and determination			
Inspire the trust of others			
Empathize with others	✔	✔	✔
Organize others	✔	✔	✔

Time needed: up to 1 hour

How to

There are three stages to this:

1 Model the conscience role play. A, B and C. C is the conscience. Amazingly, some students will never have heard of the term and unsurprisingly no one has a very clear definition, part of the point of this game is to get leaders thinking about it.

   Use a role play like this: A is a storekeeper. B is a shopper. B walks into the store and asks for a packet of sweets. The storekeeper has to turn her back leaving the counter untended. Make it more difficult by supposing there is no CCTV. C, the conscience, tries his best to stop B from doing anything wrong. B can argue back as much as she likes. C can appeal to the group for help.

2 Break out into trios. Play out a similar situation. Ones that work well include:
- A knows she has lost the iPod lent to her by B. C has to persuade A to tell the truth.
- A knows he has forgotten his homework. C has to persuade A to tell the truth to the teacher.
- A has been insolent to a parent at home. C tries to get A to own up and put it right with B, the parent.

3 Hot-seat the consciences of all the trio dramas. Get the group to use the word lead or leadership in their questions, like: 'Why did you lead in the way you did? What leadership did you give?'

Challenge

This is a seriously difficult challenge. Give plenty of support to the volunteer – and it must be a volunteer. Tell her you are going to put a great deal of trust and respect in this person's ability. When you've got a volunteer – and you will after a build up such as this – get the group to give a power clap. (Incidentally, this can have an unexpectedly helpful effect when it is three, sharp, clean single claps rather than the usual round of applause. It becomes their applause. Anything that gives the group a sense of difference from others is helpful, especially when trying to turn around poor self-esteem.) One person becomes the group conscience. Role play: a supply teacher arrives to take the class. A student takes this role. The group are a class who will take advantage of this situation. Give the 'supply teacher' some basic content: adding up two and two, will do.

The class gives the supply teacher a few challenges.

The leader conscience stops the drama with the command 'I'm using the command – change'. You make sure the drama is governed by this rule: everything stops on that word.

Teach a few power projection skills:

- Address the group with an assertive voice – use the consonants of your instruction – 'I'm using the command – change'.
- Choose a power position in the room, right at the front, sufficiently far back to see everyone but not too far back to look unimportant.
- Use power eye contact (holding eye contact for a fraction of second longer than is socially necessary).
- Keep your stillness. Don't rock back and forth.

Then have the group conscience tell the class how they should **feel, imagine and think. The acronym FIT has become a thread through much of the role play done.** Ask the class to think about what they are doing; to imagine what could be different; to say what the supply teacher might be feeling.

FIT is a good way to structure the challenge of being the **group conscience**. It lets you get into what the cross-overs are between the leader and the conscience of the group, class, family or school.

Katy – Student voice

Seeing my friends become the conscience of the group was an eye opener. They said things and did things I've not seen. It was as if doing the drama gave them the excuse to be someone with more courage.

We talked about whether this could be us in real life. Most of us said we'd have a go. And in the next session we reported back how this exact situation had come about: a supply teacher losing control. Not many people had tried to help in the past but most of us said we'd had a go. There's something about being the group conscience that gives you protection, like a shield. And because most of us are with two or three other learning to lead students, you aren't alone.

Discussion points

- Is there a conscience?
- Where does it come from?
- How can you get one if you think you don't have one already?

Leadership tip

The leader can be the conscience of the group. The leader can help others develop a conscience by asking questions, wondering aloud and being assertive about what's right and wrong.

One of the most common definitions used came from the students: **conscience is the inner leader**. This makes sense to many groups and also adults.

Helping each other in class make a difference is so important. One of the definitions of an outstanding ethos in schools is: students arrive in class asking themselves and their fellow students and teacher **'How can I help?'** Something as simple as this is so rare and is a key indicator that a radical shift has taken place in the learning culture. So seek it, celebrate it and feel rightly proud when you have helped this come about.

Activity 44: The personal challenge

This activity allows students to plan an aspect of personal leadership and get positive constructive feedback.

Positive influence over others	Positive influence over yourself		
	Using your personal integrity	Organize yourself	Use your ambition to motivate yourself
Give instructions to help a group task	✔	✔	✔
Guide other people	✔	✔	✔
Question to secure a task objective			
Set an example	✔	✔	✔
Take a longer-term view of things	✔	✔	✔
Take the initiative	✔	✔	✔
Show courage and determination	✔	✔	✔
Inspire the trust of others	✔	✔	✔
Empathize with others	✔	✔	✔
Organize others	✔	✔	✔

Time needed: 30 minutes to describe and plan

How to

Tell students this is leadership in action. They are going to plan, deliver and assess their leadership skills. The personal challenge time limit should be no longer than three weeks. This is usually set in the mid part of the course, once students have built up enough skills to be successful. Examples of personal challenges are as below:

- To keep my mathematics book tidy, well organized and to act on all the marking given me; to make sure I complete all the homework I am set and to ask if I don't understand the activity.
- To help my brother with his reading at home. To read with him twice a week for three weeks. I will help him choose a book, let him do some reading to me and help him if he gets stuck.

Learning to Lead © Graham Tyrer (Continuum 2010)

- To ask my parents at least once a day whether there is anything I can do to help at home and to show them my planner.
- To ask a teacher at least once a week whether there is anything I can do to help in the lesson.
- To help someone in a lesson at least twice week, and, if I can, for this to be someone I don't really know.
- To plan, with my family, an outing at the weekend. I will organize the food, plan the route and check everyone is having a good time at the event.

We give choices like these around home and school. Make sure that students have personal challenges that take them into comfort zone plus and that they have the support of their family or teacher.

Students choose two of the leadership objectives to have assessed. They choose the person who will be assessing them. They secure this person's agreement. These acts of personal leadership are as important as the activity itself. For students to plan, seek agreement and choose the criteria against which they will be assessed is a sign that they are making progress towards better personal leadership.

The challenges are relative: for some students, getting homework completed and in on time is a significant achievement. So care needs to be taken that they have had guidance in choosing the right level of demand. Ask them to draft out their first thoughts and you can review and amend where necessary. But it is also important they have a sense of ownership.

The timescale should be short. This is for several reasons: it means it is easier for the students to see an end date; it is easier for you to track success and give help where necessary and it helps the students' motivation. So, in three to four weeks, completion can be celebrated.

The involvement of other teachers and family members in the assessment is important and creates a sense of community support for the students.

Challenge

At an advanced level, students can publicise what they have done by speaking in an assembly or even to the staff of the school at a staff briefing.

There are strong positive outcomes to such a challenge. Often this is the first time staff or other students have heard such self-motivated talk from the student. The students gain essential positive feedback from staff and other students and it raises their profile as an emergent leader. It adds to the sense that something important is happening in the students' learning.

There's more opportunity to discuss the paralinguistics of presentation (e.g. stillness, eye contact, voice projection, clarity of diction) and the discourse markers of leadership presentation, from formal, inclusive greetings to the group, a description of what they did and what they achieved, and the enrichment of their vocabulary by using the leadership objectives.

Tatyana – Student voice

When I talked to the staff meeting, even though it was short piece, I was nervous and I didn't know what they would think. But they gave me applause and smiled – I didn't expect that. And then, for the rest of that week, teachers kept coming up and saying how well I had done and some said they didn't know I could do it.

My challenge was to help my sister with her homework. She's in Year 7 so a lot of what she's doing, I have done. I got her to assess me. I had to talk to her about whether I had **taken the initiative** and whether I had **organized her**. She thought I had and she wanted me to keep helping her and so I do, whenever I have the time and I didn't before.

Learning to Lead © Graham Tyrer (Continuum 2010)

Getting the form filled in was part of the challenge. I've got lots of homework of my own to do and this had to be done too. But because it was only a three-week challenge it wasn't too difficult. Anyway, that's why it's called a challenge. And I got to help someone I don't usually help in that way.

Discussion points

- What do you think you need to improve?
- What kind of activity might help you improve it?
- Who might be the best person to help?
- How will you explain how to assess the activity? Role play this. Explain the purpose; explain the learning objectives.

Leadership tip

This is leadership in action in everyday life. We use it as an important part of the course. To get something out of leadership learning in a workshop is so important but applying the skills in life makes the learning memorable and gives even greater impetus to subsequent workshops.

Activity 45: Leading your learning style – learning-style log

Track the way students learn and improve the way they lead their learning.

Positive influence over others	Positive influence over yourself		
	Using your personal integrity	Organize yourself	Use your ambition to motivate yourself
Give instructions to help a group task	✔	✔	✔
Guide other people			
Question to secure a task objective			
Set an example			
Take a longer-term view of things	✔	✔	✔
Take the initiative	✔	✔	✔
Show courage and determination	✔	✔	✔
Inspire the trust of others	✔	✔	✔
Empathize with others	✔	✔	✔
Organize others	✔	✔	✔

Time needed: 30 minutes and then periodically. Each learning log entry and feedback can take as little as 10 minutes

How to

Introduce students to the idea of learning styles. Three theories are usually enough. The idea is to engage students with the idea of learning theory, at challenge level, to invent their own style. This is where the leadership of learning becomes seriously exciting. Having students learn the content of learning theory, debate, contest, enquire and adapt, and then readapt according to the influence of time and situation and content, is right at the heart of learning leadership.

Three theories that can be introduced to students are:

- **Transmission theory**
- **Multiple intelligence theory**
- **Whole brain theory.**

For each activity, use three steps.

First: introduce three main ideas about the theory.

Second: teach this to someone else.

Third: plenary through a **TRA learning log: think, reflect and act**. Students keep these logs in writing or on their VLE e-portfolio as pieces of digital video, mind maps or discursive prose, as they see fit.

It's worth saying that two of the driving ideas behind the pedagogy of this work are:

Curiosity: when students are helped to be leaders they become curious; they take an important step along the road to becoming an outstanding learner and leader. Curiosity is the first step. Without that there can be no progression, no challenge. So, the theories presented were offered in a taster form; make sure student are curious enough to **debate, discuss and enquire (DDE)**.

Choice: the assumption is that there is no such thing as a fixed learning style. That is, it's more positive to invite students to make active choices about the kind of learning styles they want to adopt. The vision is: **a learning leader asks these questions: 'What skill, knowledge or attitude do I need to learn? How shall I co-construct the learning methods to learn the content I need.'** A number of assumptions need to be explained here. Leading learners will take have to know what they are capable of and this will be a demand they create themselves. In simple terms, they ask, what's my target and how can I get there? This is a leading learning prerequisite and has to be done in consultation with the teacher. When that's done, the leading learner finds out what knowledge attitudes or skills he needs. When he's done that, he applies the metacognitive skills at the heart of this work. E.g.: suppose he knows that he needs to learn the semi-colon to improve the quality of his extended writing. **The leading learner asks:**

- **'How shall I learn this?'**
- **'With whom shall I learn this?'**
- **'How will I know I have learned it?'** We call these **learning scripts.** They are discourse markers telling us that the leading learners are making progress as leading learners.

At a challenge level, leaders are also asking:

- **'Who am I learning this for?'**
- '**Who will benefit?'**
- **'What positive changes will happen in my life, my community and even in the wider regional, global context?'** We encourage, throughout, the belief that whatever you do, wherever you do it, has consequences way beyond your current context.

So the content: the learning theories.

These are offered as *three lists of ten assertions*. Take each in turn and teach them in three different ways to the whole group that has been grouped into A, B and C.

Group A would be taught using transmission theory.

Group B would be taught using some of the principles of the whole brain theory, for example as a simple statement game, inviting the students to rank the assertions in the order they find most important.

Group C would be taught using one of the assertions of multiple intelligences. So, for example, they would be asked to choose two styles, combine them and present the theory to the class. They might offer the theory as a TV chat show, with a learning scientist being interviewed about what the theory contains and how useful it might be. This would combine the kinesthetic and linguistic intelligence.

After this introductory work, there is plenty of discussion, learning log and practice to explore. Follow up activities include:

Debate in small groups the relative merits of these theories. Make it clear they have contentious elements within them all. What often happens is that leaders decide they like some parts of some theories. What's important is that they are in the metacognitive domain, but make clear that this is key.

Keep a week-long learning log. This is a very simple activity where students record, in words or multimedia, the learning that has been most effective during the five days of their enquiry. They write about what made the activity memorable or intriguing or provoking curiosity.

Challenge

You are not asking students to choose *between* the theories **but to choose *from* them** and, at an advanced level, to invent their own methods of retaining knowledge, skills and attitudes. **This is when real learning leadership has begun.**

Have the students ask the teacher if they can design a short sequence of teaching for a small group or even the whole class. A good idea for this is asking students to think about delivering a ten-minute starter. Most colleague teachers will usually go along with this. It saves them a little work and helps make a key piece of their content memorable and interesting to the rest of the class.

This really takes root. Student leaders want to go on and design PowerPoint® materials, set independent study activities and even design rewards and ask for feed back on their teaching.

The key is to invite leaders to plan for short teaching sequences lasting no longer than 20 minutes. It's a highly skilled activity after all; often students will say it has been a revelation to understand what goes into planning and delivering a lesson.

Michael – Student voice

We invented a new activity with the theory content. We mixed all 30 of the statements up together and then decided which were the top ten. This gave a new theory and we felt proud that we have taken the best of them and come up with something new and something that could be tried out on others.

It was interesting that no one had the same top ten. It showed us that no one theory applied to everyone. We are all different according to who we are, when we learn, where we learn and what we learn. That makes it important to lead your learning. You have to know what you could do to be adaptable and not so dependent on the teacher.

We liked using the terms metacognition and multiple intelligences and, although we didn't agree with everything, we thought and planned how learning could stick.

Discussion points

- When you make progress in a lesson, what made it happen? Reflect on what the teacher did, what you did and what others were doing.
- Do you learn differently according to your mood, the content of the lesson, the time of day, the day of the week?
- How can you make use of this knowledge to take more control over your learning?
- Are there other intelligences to add to Gardner's list?
- Are there other ways your mind works to add to the whole brain theory?
- Are there ways of transmitting knowledge that can be engaging and entertaining?

Learning to Lead © Graham Tyrer (Continuum 2010)

Leadership tip

It is so important that the student leaders engage in the debate. It raises many issues for educators. Leading learners debate, think and design learning activities to suit particular purposes. The work in this activity leads students away from the notion that we have fixed attitudes, intelligences or skills. It is an exciting revelation to many student leaders that they can work with teachers, others students and parents to invent ways of making progress.

Basic learning theory content: three lists of ten assertions
Transmission teaching

Often called 'traditional teaching' this is felt by many teachers to be efficient. It allows the teacher to get over key knowledge, attitudes and skills quickly and to large groups.

Teachers who use transmission theory do the following:

1 They present the content of the lesson without debate or much discussion.
2 The lesson is mostly teacher talk.
3 Students do an activity after they have heard from the teacher.
4 The teacher is almost always one of the teaching staff, although sometimes it is an expert from outside school.
5 This style is sometimes called a 'lecture'.
6 Sometimes students are asked to take notes during the teaching.
7 There is often a homework set at the end.
8 Teaching like this can form the whole of a lesson or part of a lesson. When it is part of a lesson it can take up most, some or a very short section of the lesson.
9 Students believe that the teacher is the 'knowledge, attitude or skill expert' and they 'receive' knowledge or attitudes or skills.
10 The teacher will often use textbooks, the internet and/or worksheets in the teaching.

Whole brain theory

Teachers who use this theory have studied what is believed about the way the brain works. Knowledge of the way the brain learns is developing all the time and by no means agreed on. These ten assertions are commonly agreed on but this does not make them completely true.

What do you think?

1 The brain's three primary senses are visual, auditory and kinesthetic.
2 For learning content to stick, all three major learning senses must be involved; that is, you must hear something explained, see the content in visual form and do a physical activity using, for example, movement, dance, acting or role play.
3 Part of the brain, called the amygdala responds well to rewards and praise. So, giving rewards and praise often, when deserved, 'feeds' this part of the brain.
4 The part of the brain most closely associated with long-term memory, called the hippocampus, is closely linked to the emotional centres of the brain called the limbic cortex. So, when we stimulate positive, optimistic feelings at the same time as learning content, it is more likely to be remembered for longer.
5 The 'oldest' part of the brain in terms of evolution, is called the cerebellum. This controls our basic unconscious activities such as need for food, drink, warmth and security. So, ensuring the

learner feels in a secure classroom, with predictable routines and rituals is more likely to help learning take place for longer.

6   The brain responds to threat or anxiety in what is known as 'fight or flight' modes. To prevent either extreme in learning, the lesson has to have opportunities for security, safety and routine.

7   Since most of the brain is composed of water, regular hydration is essential for learning.

8   The most recent part of the brain, in terms of evolution, is called the neocortex. This is the outer surface of the brain. It controls higher-order thinking. For this part of the brain to work effectively, all the other parts of the brain, such as the limbic system, the cerebellum and the amygdala have to be stimulated positively.

9   Positive visualization can help learning. When the mind sees, hears and uses other senses to imagine a positive outcome, it is easier to think of ways to bring these outcomes about.

10 The brain's effectiveness is increased when clear goals are set. This is why target setting can help, especially when challenging but realistic and short term.

Multiple intelligence theory

This stems from, among others, a researcher called Howard Gardner. He suggested we have many more than the commonly understood notions of intelligence. Well known to most educators, it is new to many students.

What do you think?

1   Visual: you remember ideas and knowledge through seeing picture and diagrams. You enjoy working through moving or still images. You find you see in images and often use words or phrases that incorporate language of sight, such as 'I see what you mean,' 'I can see in my mind's eye.'

2   Auditory: you can recall clearly what was said to you. You enjoy listening to someone explain an idea or concept. You can repeat what has been said closely to the original. If a teacher says, 'listen' or 'pay attention to what I am going to say', you enjoy it and feel safe.

3   Kinesthetic: you enjoy activities such as dance, drama and sports. You can invent shapes, mimes and movements. You enjoy it when the teacher says, 'now get into role', or 'would you like to make up a short play or dance or physical game?'

4   Linguistic: you have a way with words. You enjoy activities such as writing, learning new vocabulary, word play and telling stories. When a teacher says, 'I'd like you to write the answer to these questions', or 'describe this experiment' or 'explain in your own words what you have just seen', anything that involves writing with a pen or word processor, you respond positively to.

5   Logical: you enjoy solving puzzles. You are good with numbers. You like the challenge of a game involving problem solving, inference and deduction. You can analyse a problem piece by piece and predict a solution based on evidence you have put together. You like the abstract of number. You like the challenge and success of algebra, for instance, or making and solving equations.

6   Interpersonal: you know how to solve problems between people; you understand how to help people when they need help; you have an intuitive understanding of people's motives and beliefs. You use your skills of empathy. You find that people turn to you to ask for advice. You are what is commonly understood a 'people person'.

7   Intrapersonal: you do not mind learning on your own. Often you prefer it. You understand your own emotions and think about them much of the time. You have a good emotional vocabulary; you may keep a personal diary; you may enjoy talking about your own emotions and thoughts

to other people. You know how to think through your own emotional situation and enjoy exploring your thoughts and feelings.

8 Musical: you learn using music and rhythm. You find you can remember tunes, songs and jingles. You put lesson content to music: if you have to recall a set of history facts, for example, you can turn them into a song and you find this helps in tests.

9 Spatial: you enjoy using space and design. You can work in three dimensions with sculpture, resistant materials or two-dimensional planning. If asked to recall science facts for a test, you enjoy building a model on paper or on CAD that represents the content, say a molecular structure.

10 Naturalistic: you have an interest in the way natural things grow and are sustained. You enjoy working with living things, understanding how we care for them, look after their ecosystems and how living things are interdependent. So, when you have to remember, say, geography knowledge, you can represent it in your notes in organic form, as a growing design, a thought map for example, that develops and takes on new ideas in the same way as natural growth occurs.

Activity 46: Learning walk

Students think about what they learn and how they learn it.

Positive influence over others	**Positive influence over yourself**		
	Using your personal integrity	Organize yourself	Use your ambition to motivate yourself
Give instructions to help a group task	✔	✔	✔
Guide other people	✔	✔	✔
Question to secure a task objective	✔	✔	✔
Set an example			
Take a longer-term view of things			
Take the initiative			
Show courage and determination			
Inspire the trust of others			
Empathize with others	✔	✔	✔
Organize others	✔	✔	✔

Time needed: 20 minutes

How to

Say: 'This game will help you think about how you can mix learning styles to help you learn something.' Students need to have done some basic preparation; it's important this happens for the activity but also as a sign that they are leading their own learning. Students ask a science teacher for the next aspect of their learning they need in order to make progress. 'What's my next step? What do I really need to understand and practice?' This element of practice is key, especially in science.

Then, in the activity, post four learning styles posters, one in each corner of the room. They can be:

- **kinesthetic**
- **linguistic**

Learning to Lead © Graham Tyrer (Continuum 2010)

- **musical**
- **visual.**

Then model for them how to stand between or close to one or other of the styles. So, if you think kinesthetic will dominate your learning activity, you go and stand very close to that poster.

If you think you are more musical and visual, you stand between these two posters.

If you think a mixture of all four, you stand in the middle of the room equidistant to each poster.

What's happening is that you are inviting them to make choices and think about learning. They are leading their own learning by thinking of alternatives, selecting, combining and being curious. There's no pressure because they don't have to think of the activity, simply think through what might work.

Challenge

What happens is that students will have grouped together in various areas of the room: some more to one or other of the corners. Some between two or three styles. So, now invite them to develop a ten-minute activity in the groups they have formed. Those who want to mix music with visual, might invent a rap and an mp3 image for downloading.

You can go a step further and involve more than four posters. Here, start as before but with posters of nine learning styles. There are examples of the kinds of activities they might invent in the linked website. This is based on a sequence of science content. Again, they first choose where to stand between the different styles. It's much more challenging because the choice is so broad. But the thinking, evident as they look, read, choose and select a place to stand, is fascinating. Seeing students edge a metre this way or that as they think:

- **What would help me learn this content?**
- **How could I combine one activity with another?**
- **Who could help me adapt the activity?**
- **There are few more important thinking steps a learning leader can take than these.** And the more they get into the habit of reflecting on and challenging this model, the more of a leading learner they will become.

Aadarsh – Student voice

It felt different being asked to stand between learning styles but you really felt that was the point. You found yourself pulled in one direction or another. And that's the point. You aren't fixed. Later in the session I would have felt differently, tomorrow differently, with an English lesson or geography, different too. What we learned was that there are more choices than you realize and the more you get involved in thinking about this, the more you lead and the more you learn.

Discussion points

- Did you choose activities because they were easy or because they would help you remember your content? What is the difference between easy and effective? Students will get engaged in this level of metalearning talk. And, if challenged, they will challenge themselves to choose effective over easy.
- How did you lead others when you were inventing a learning activity? What strengths did you draw on? What strengths did you need? What's happening, that's so important, is that leaders in some areas of strength, drama or mind mapping, say are sharing those skills with others to create hybrid activities that others can use. This is real learning leadership: interdependent leadership.

Leadership tip

The more you do this kind of metacognitive leadership work, the more you find colleagues of these students telling you how active students are becoming in their lessons. And this is what we want. A culture where students leading their own and co-leading others' learning by becoming learning tinkers and learning developers.

This is the resource we use to explore learning style and learning activity leadership. Anything that has content similar to the kind of knowledge students expected to retain for tests and exams will do. It's the process of learning that is being focused on.

Exemplary science content knowledge

Our solar system consists of the Sun and nine planets orbiting (or moving around) the Sun.

- Four inner planets (closest to the Sun) Mercury, Venus, Earth, Mars.
- Five outer planets (further from the Sun) Jupiter, Saturn, Uranus, Neptune, Pluto.
- All the planets move in elliptical orbits in the same direction around the Sun.
- Unlike stars, planets do not give off their own light – they reflect light from the Sun.
- Planets closer to the Sun will have a shorter orbit time than the planets further from the Sun.
- For instance, Mercury takes 88 days to orbit the Sun, while Pluto takes 248 years! Thus you can see that a planet's orbit time will depend on its distance from the Sun.
- As a planet's distance from the Sun increases, so will its orbit time.

See the table below for **challenge** information about the planets.

Planet	Distance from the sun (in millions of km)	Radius (km)	Average surface temperature (°C)
Mercury	58	2,400	450
Venus	108	6,025	500
Earth	149	6,350	20
Mars	227	3,360	−40
Jupiter	778	70,960	−150
Saturn	1,427	+/−60,000	−160
Uranus	2,870	24,500	−220
Neptune	4,490	25,000	−230
Pluto	5,900	+/−3,000	−230

Possible learning activities
Interpersonal

Devise a 'Who Wants to Be a Millionaire?' 'fastest finger first' set of six questions about the planets. E.g.: 'Put the planets in the correct order starting with the hottest.'

Intrapersonal

On your own:

- Choose a word that reflects your feelings about each of the planets.
- Which of the planets might sustain any form of life? Why?

- Which planets could not possibly sustain any form of life? Why?
- If it were possible to visit any of the planets, which would you choose and why?

Kinesthetic

Devise a short role-play scene in which the planets meet in a local Galaxy Club and show off to each other about their various dimensions and proximity to the Sun.

Visual/spatial

Present the order of the planets from the Sun as a three-dimensional cut out. Use string, Blu-Tack and coloured pens as inventively as you wish. Use the space in the hall.

Naturalist

Find different ways of grouping the planets. How many different ways could you classify them?

Linguistic

Write a short but sensational newspaper article for the *Alpha Centuri Sun* in which you describe the main features of this newly discovered solar system.

Mathematical/logical

If NASA were to send a discovery probe into the solar system, what order would you suggest the probe visit the planets? Give reasons.

How long would it take for the probe to return to Earth, even if the probe travelled at a constant speed of .1 of the speed of light?

Musical/rhythmic

Devise a rap to explain the order of the planets from the sun and any other information about surface temperatures.

Activity 47: Leadership theatre role plays

Students solve real-life problems around them, with others, leading others.

Positive influence over others	Positive influence over yourself		
	Using your personal integrity	Organize yourself	Use your ambition to motivate yourself
Give instructions to help a group task	✔	✔	✔
Guide other people	✔	✔	✔
Question to secure a task objective	✔	✔	✔
Set an example			
Take a longer-term view of things			
Take the initiative			
Show courage and determination			
Inspire the trust of others	✔	✔	✔
Empathize with others	✔	✔	✔
Organize others	✔	✔	✔

Time needed: up to 1 hour

How to

Tell the leaders: 'You have a responsibility to get involved in the lives of others, if you can help. You should do no harm. Leave well alone if you think you could do more harm than good. But don't walk away from someone who needs your help.'

Set up a simple role play, modelled for the class. For example: asking your best friend for help with homework and you are worried about appearing uncool.

Set some ground rules. Tell the audience they can change the course of the drama whenever they want. They can lead the situation whenever they want. To take control, they say, '**pause**'. The drama stops and students can suggest something else someone might say. Or they can change places with someone else. If this is to be done, you stop the drama with the word '**change**'.

Challenge

Invite students to choose a role-play situation they have actually experienced. They can draft these up on slips of paper. They can choose a domestic or school event. Keep them safe by reminding them that no one has to reveal a painful or distressing event. It might be a time when they were confused or puzzled. Or when better leadership might have provided a solution. Remind them that the moment we role play might seem almost trivial: a disagreement in the lunch queue, a lost pen in lesson. If students want to take it further and explore deeper, more resonant moments, then that's their choice.

Be clear that their event may not be chosen from the secret box you use. 'You might be relieved to know that not everyone's event can be chosen. It's the luck of the draw.'

Katy – Student voice

We used 'pause' and 'change' a lot because it's great getting involved in the drama and not just watching it. We talked about how this is what leaders do. They get involved. Someone said, 'leaders don't play in the sidelines, they play on the pitch'. And that's how it feels when you step into the drama and no one minds if they give way. They can back in whenever they want.

Sometimes we call this drama, tag drama. We suggested dividing in two teams and one half of the group helps one character; the other half supports the other person. It's good because it makes it competitive. Makes more of game out of it.

Someone else called this dramaplus because you can pause and rewind, hold the action and talk. But what you can't do on TV is change what happened. In this game you can.

Discussion points

- What does it mean to be cool?
- Who gets to decide this?
- How can we change what others think is cool? Students will suggest routes; they say things such as: 'don't worry what others think/it's none of their business/you're working for yourself not them'.

One of the most powerful things someone said was: '**your grades are for the children who haven't been born yet**'. This line has become a strong thread through learning to lead. **Leaders are working in the present for the future.**

Leadership tip

Work hard at the image of the leader. Get leaders to see positive change as 'cool'. The concept of leadership will help in doing this. Fortunately it has strong resonance for most young people. So when the drama is stopped, saying 'OK, lead it,' helps raise the status of getting involved. Standing by and watching became uncool.

Chose situations such as:

- **Asking a teacher for help reaching your grade target.**
- **Helping someone who seemed to have difficulty in class.**
- **Getting someone in the class to stop interrupting the teacher.**

Activity 48: Learning leaders

Using plenary role cards will help in leading learning in your school lessons.

Positive influence over others	Positive influence over yourself		
	Using your personal integrity	Organize yourself	Use your ambition to motivate yourself
Give instructions to help a group task	✔	✔	✔
Guide other people	✔	✔	✔
Question to secure a task objective			
Set an example	✔	✔	✔
Take a longer-term view of things			
Take the initiative			
Show courage and determination			
Inspire the trust of others	✔	✔	✔
Empathize with others			
Organize others			

Time needed: 30 minutes to explain; about 10 minutes in subsequent sessions to get feedback and improve skills

How to

This can radically change the way classrooms are led. Using the **plenary role cards** (see online resource sheet: Plenary role cards) will help students in leading learning in their school lessons and the learning of themselves and other students.

Place about three **role cards** face down on the chairs or desks of three students before they come into the room. When they see a card, they know this is their leadership role for the lesson. You explain what to do. Each card's 'scripts' are given on the following pages. You can print these on the back of the card. The cards can be any size you like, although they do work well in playing card size.

The assessor – Use the DLOs and or level descriptors to find any good or exceptional progress.	During the lesson, ask students what progress they have made towards the learning objectives. Have they understood the DLOs (DLOs are differentiated learning objectives, e.g. must, should, could). This is better done talking to students on a one to one basis. Ask them what they think they need next. Feedback to the teacher so she can plan what to offer next to the class and to individuals.
The chair – Make sure everyone is included, listens well and keeps to time.	'Your job is to lead any whole class discussions that take place, for example during the plenary. Keep everyone involved. Use the "thinking time trick", call on people only after they've had time to think. And remember you don't have to ask people whose hands are up. Try getting people to talk in small groups or pairs before responding. You may be asked to manage time in the lesson: the teacher may ask you to remind her when it's time for the plenary. You may be invited to chair this part of the lesson.'
The questioner – Ask at least three open questions and two closed questions: who and what.	During the lesson, ask three questions about the lesson topic. Question to make sure the class has understood the lesson content. If you can, ask questions that encourage curiosity. Ask something to which you'd really like an answer. An open question is one to which there could be many answers. A closed question usually has very few right answers, such as 'What's your name?' An open version of this could be: 'What do you think of your name?' Open questions usually get people thinking.
The greeter – If a guest comes to the room, greet him, welcome him and ask if you can tell him what we are learning today.	If someone comes into the room, stand and greet them. Say, 'Good morning. Welcome to our lesson.' If you are feeling brave, say, 'Can I tell you what we are learning today?' this will remind everyone in the room what they are achieving today.
The celebrator – In the plenary, find two examples of people working well together or producing high-quality learning.	'During the lesson, keep a look out for anything that needs rewarding. In particular, look for examples of people achieving things they used to find difficult. Look for brave learners, learners stepping into comfort zone plus. Your job is to lead the celebration. Encourage polite applause. Let the class know what you think has been done well. Get the permission of your nominees first.'

Learning to Lead © Graham Tyrer (Continuum 2010)

The literacy coordinator – Find any two examples of people using high-quality language.	'You are looking for language that's accurate. You are also looking for people who have made an effort, say, to expand their specialist vocabulary or tried to spell a word they find difficult. You might find good handwriting. Some people may have written more than three paragraphs or used varied connectives. There might be examples of flair and imagination in writing or talk.'
The learning to learn assessor – Find any two examples of people learning well; how were they doing this?	'Lead the class learning self-assessment. Has anyone tried to take responsibility for their own learning? Has anyone suggested different ways of learning the lesson content? Has anyone thought through what would work for them? Has anyone tried to help the group or another student overcome any difficulty?'
The target leader – Ask any three people how close they are to their personal target.	'Lead the class' sense of aspiration. 'Ask whether anyone knows their target. Ask whether anyone has made progress towards this. Ask whether anyone knows what they need to do next. Your teacher will have suggestions and so will others in the class.'
The numeracy coordinator – Find two examples of people using numbers well.	'Lead the group's interest in numbers and learning through number. Has anyone used statistics accurately? Has anyone found a way of learning a mathematical equation they think works? Has anyone used numbers in an original way, for instance applied mathematics to an artistic or literary question? Some people might have tried making a graph to track the emotions of a character in a poem or story.'
The emotional literacy leader – What emotions were important today?	'Lead the class reflection on emotions used in the lesson.' This is better done in the middle of the lesson so the class can change the emotional atmosphere to help the learning. Following are a few examples:

- Cheerfulness
- Contentment
- Disappointment
- Enthrallment
- Exasperation
- Irritation
- Nervousness
- Optimism
- Pride
- Relief
- Sadness
- Surprise
- Sympathy
- Zest.

Challenge

Getting other staff involved builds a momentum. This strategy can have a widespread impact. It depends on the culture of your school and the colleagues who are willing to work with you. But this can really catch on. Once it has been taught to the group, they are able to go into a staff meeting and let colleagues know what they have been trained to do. The cards were then made available to staff to use voluntarily. Staff reported it made a virtue out of the inevitable interruptions to lessons. More important, the leadership ethos spread.

Gradually, you can withdraw the card because you have made this kind of leadership routine. This means you have stepped up the quality of learning. **Once students come to expect they will be leading learning, you have made a significant cultural step forward.**

Michael – Student voice

The most popular was the greeter. It's quite a challenge to stand up and tell a visitor what we are learning. But it does make you think about what the lesson's about and it reminds the class what they are supposed to be achieving. There's a real sense that it's not just the teacher making things happen and changing things for the better in the lesson. Too often students just sit there. But having **lesson leaders** like this remind us **if it's to be, it's down to me**.

Discussion point

- In role play, try out the leadership styles you'll need to make this work. How can you encourage people, for instance, to tell you what they think they need to learn next? Try asking questions. Start with closed questions, so you encourage confidence. For instance: 'What are you learning?' 'Where are you up to?' Then become more open, getting your fellow students to do some reflection and thinking. For instance: 'Do you think you have made any progress?' 'How can you tell?' 'What do you think you need to do next?' 'How could you find out?'

Leadership tip

Students' learning is more likely to be retained in a classroom ethos where students take responsibility. Lessons where this strategy is used are more welcoming, proactive and effective.

You might find it helps to prepare for this with an explanation to the staff with the students' assistance if you can. It helps for staff to see it working. And there's nothing more effective than hearing students tell the staff how it is helping them make progress.

The activity is a good way to get leadership widespread through your school. You will find students and staff talk about what they are doing. **You'll find that students are much less passive and expect to lead.**

Activity 49: The group challenge

This will help students improve their skills of practical leadership. Work together to improve the life of your school or community.

Positive influence over others	Positive influence over yourself		
	Using your personal integrity	Organize yourself	Use your ambition to motivate yourself
Give instructions to help a group task	✔	✔	✔
Guide other people	✔	✔	✔
Question to secure a task objective	✔	✔	✔
Set an example	✔	✔	✔
Take a longer-term view of things	✔	✔	✔
Take the initiative	✔	✔	✔
Show courage and determination	✔	✔	✔
Inspire the trust of others	✔	✔	✔
Empathize with others	✔	✔	✔
Organize others	✔	✔	✔

Time needed: about 40 minutes to prepare

How to

Say: 'First you will need to choose a number of things: who your leadership team will be; what you want to lead; which assessment objectives each of you want; who will assess you.' The impact of this activity can be significant around the school and community. Even in a group of 30 students, there can be six or seven group challenges all happening at the same time of the year over a short period. Six weeks make the challenges manageable and increase the intensity of the effect: to create a sense of urgency, of change happening, of leadership in action.

Say: 'This is an opportunity to change things for the better, to prove to others what you are capable of, to **make others proud of you**.'

Give examples of group challenges. These include:

Plan, publicise, run and evaluate an IT club running once a week for six week for Year 7 students.

In this challenge, students put posters up. They go into Year 7 assembly to sell the course they are running, they talk with the IT teacher about the lesson planning she did and then use her blank lesson proformas to plan their lessons. They produce certificates for the students who come along and even write a simple evaluation for their clients to complete, in which they have to say what they have learned and whether they enjoy the sessions.

Plan and organize three visits to a local primary school to help encourage reading.

Students make the phone calls, liaise with staff to plan the trips and work out what books they should take and share. They have choice over the reading they want to celebrate. One year, students did this in role as the authors, getting the students in a circle, sharing the parts of the books they liked the most and encouraging questions. **Learning is about curiosity.** Say to the students that if they have done this they have helped the students take a significant step forward. They are not teachers of reading: you cannot expect those skills. But fascination, intrigue, questions are all aspects of learning tht young leaders can help encourage.

Take charge of an area of the school. Make sure the displays in the corridor are well maintained and the students who use the corridor treat it with respect.

In one example, students worked with the PE staff to take charge of a noticeboard. It may not sound like much, but the work involved finding all the materials for displays, arranging them, maintaining them and ensuring no one damaged the display for six weeks, which was something of an accomplishment. It helped the leaders understand how even apparently easy processes in school life involve high levels of commitment, an investment in time, a sense of pride and require the allegiance of their peers. Afterwards, these students had a new respect for staff and their work around the school. They told us that they recognized how much they had taken for granted around the school.

Challenge

Use the assessment sheets provided on the website.

Have the students systematically evaluate and pan their work. As with the personal challenge this is about students leading their own learning. By making decisions over the process, the learning objectives and the people they think can assess them, they are embedding key leadership skills and becoming better leaders. We normally place this group challenge towards the end of the course so they are ready for the responsibility and there can be a sense around the school that a difference has been made because of the learning students have gone through.

Tatyana – Student voice

Planning a lesson was really interesting. Thinking about what we wanted the students to get out of it at the end and then working out what we could do in the lunchtime lessons was really interesting. It's hard standing up in front of a class even when they all want to be there. It must be so tough if they don't. We worked in a group so we could pass the jobs around. One of us gave the introduction and welcomed the students. Someone else told the group what they would be learning and we all worked with them on their computers. Finding out what they thought at the end was great. There was a real feeling that they had enjoyed it and got something from it. And it made us feel important that we were asking them what they thought. We thought this too: we think we should be asked more often how we could improve lessons. Sometimes we don't know but sometimes we do. One of the things we learn through learning to lead is that we have the skills to help. We can help the lessons go better.

Teaching a lesson to younger students showed me what it's like to be a teacher and made us more willing to tell teachers we could help them in their lessons

Discussion points

- What went well?
- What would you do differently?
- What do you think you could improve with others?
- What do you think you could improve in a team that you couldn't do alone? This is key. Often students have conception that leadership is about being alone. However, leadership in synergy has as much if not more potential.
- What difference have you made?
- How can you help make this difference last? This is also key. When a leader makes a change, she improves the strength and capacity of others. This is about personal improvement. But what we try to teach is that personal improvement is dependent on the positive changes experienced by others.

Leadership tip

One of the most important things we hear students say at the end of the challenge is: 'I didn't know I could do that.' It sound simple but, in learning, this is one of the most important and difficult outcomes to reach. Leadership is about being self-reflective and taking action simultaneously. The strength of the group challenge comes from many directions. Students can see a difference. They can see how their leadership made a difference. They can begin to understand how working together in a focused, well planned and carefully evaluated way can lead to others having increased capacity.

Because you are more able, so am I changed. If you are teaching leadership for the first time, be reassured that students of even quite a young age can understand this. They want to live in happy, safe schools. They want to believe that this can happen. And, crucially, they want to believe that they can help. Even the most disaffected student wants to feel significant and we teach that leadership is about being significance, leading lives of meaning.

Activity 50: Learning parliament

An activity to show you how students' leadership can be used to change others for the better and improve their life chances. Learn how to work with others to take charge of learning and lead it for others.

Positive influence over others	Positive influence over yourself		
	Using your personal integrity	Organize yourself	Use your ambition to motivate yourself
Give instructions to help a group task	✔	✔	✔
Guide other people	✔	✔	✔
Question to secure a task objective			
Set an example	✔	✔	✔
Take a longer-term view of things			
Take the initiative			
Show courage and determination			
Inspire the trust of others	✔	✔	✔
Empathize with others	✔	✔	✔
Organize others			

Time needed: 25 minutes

How to

You set the workshop up as a **learning parliament**. Essentially, this is a debate format. Use the following debate conventions:

- a proposition is made: a speech lasting five minutes
- an opposition is given: a speech lasting five minutes
- a seconder for the proposition makes a speech lasting two minutes
- a seconder for the opposition makes a speech lasting two minutes.

Learning to Lead © Graham Tyrer (Continuum 2010)

Then speeches, questions and comments can be made from the floor.

After this has finished, each side gives a summing up speech. Then a vote is taken.

Because it's a learning parliament, we make the debates about everyday ethical, moral or learning dilemmas.

For instance

Ethical: encourage thinking about doing the right thing. Use a dilemma such as: 'You have advance information about a test. You believe you will not be found out. The debate motion is: "If you have advance information about a test, you should always tell someone".' Learning: a learning debate can be, for instance, a gender issue: It is a commonly held belief that boys' behaviour can be more challenging than girls. So, we test this out with a motion such as: 'Single sex schools would be more effective for both boys and girls.' Moral: we want our students to think through the morality of taking responsibility for others. It is a key strand of learning to lead. By so doing, questions are raised of practical solutions and how they should be reached. Students should think about, discuss and debate the issue. There is not the fault or guilt. But these issues will confront this generation. They can ignore it. Leaders challenge difficult times rather than pretend they do not exist.'It is our moral responsibility to help improve the lives of young people we do not know.'

Challenge

Participants may request a role play. This is called **thought evidence.** Any leader may set up a role play using volunteers. So, in the test scenario, two students discuss the realization that one of them has found the answers to the test. They have not stolen them but they have been found in the playground.

The role players can be **hot-seated and thought-tracked** to deepen the learning and raise more questions. The debate is resumed whenever the 'speaker' declares.

The preparation for the learning parliament is an important challenge. Students can engage in **learning enquiry**.

With the permission of staff, they can observe lessons, interview colleagues, students and keep learning logs gathering thoughts and reflections on, say, the gender question. The key is to keep such enquiry highly focused, time limited and non-judgemental. Say to students: 'You are observers. You are looking and listening. You have a responsibility to tell others what you have seen and heard.' As an example, say: **'Use the rule of three'**.'When you **observe** the learning of others, look for a maximum of *three things at a time.* Try to keep these as specific as possible. For example, student questioning, students' listening to the teacher, students' organization of their learning, e.g. their use of homework planners and their bringing the right equipment to the lesson.'When you **interview** other students, focus on only three areas. Use these fact based questions. E.g. 'When do you ask the most questions? When do you ask the least questions? What kinds of questions help you the most?'When you keep a **learning log,** make three entries a week for three weeks. Focus on three areas. For example, homework in lessons might have these enquiry areas: the most enjoyable homework; the most challenging homework; the most well explained homework.

These basic skills of enquiry – **focus, manageability, objectivity** – improve the learning leadership. They have significance for the learning parliament but they have just as much, if not more, for the wider application of leadership in and outside lessons. We believe that the more students help build an ethos of learning enquiry, the more they are contributing to an effective learning environment.

Andy – Student voice

It was important to keep the parliament debate quite formal. We found people thought more about what they said. And they said more important things than if it was just chat.

It was good to talk about difficult matters. Debating how we learn is what our everyday life is about.

Sometimes we are faced with difficult 'right and wrong' personal decisions. So debating what we should do at these times was helpful.

Thinking about whether we should try to help people we don't know is what leaders do. We all want to help our friends. But going beyond this means taking leadership seriously. We may not have answers. At least we can ask questions.

Discussion points

- What part of the **debate** was most difficult? How could it be improved? Often students say the answer is to spend more time thinking beforehand so there was more to say.
- What have you learned through doing basic **enquiry**? How could you improve your enquiry skills? Talk to other leaders about the questions they asked. Which questions got helpful responses? What do you notice about these questions? We find that students got more responses from their subjects in interviews when there was clearly no opinion evident in the questions.

Leadership tip

These debates and enquiries help leaders see their potential. We think it is important that leaders sense the importance of structured talk supported, at a challenge level, by enquiry evidence. We do not encourage false illusions but we hope students feel part of thoughtful school and community improvement.

Index

DATE DUE

JUN 1 0 2011			

GAYLORD   PRINTED IN U.S.A.